PERFECT LEADER

Andrew originally trained as an economist and later worked as a business journalist on *The Observer*. He spent many years as a senior manager in the public sector, before launching Maynard Leigh Associates with his fellow director Michael Maynard. He is the author of numerous books and articles on management and change, Teams, Leadership and Presentations, many of which have been translated around the world. He advises companies on management development programmes, particularly in the area of teams, leadership, communication, presentation and coaching. He works as a coach to senior managers and facilitates top teams in tackling major change issues. He developed the 7 I's leadership profile used by many companies to review leadership impact and improve performance.

Michael Maynard has led business and management courses all over the world, specialising in creativity, leadership, teams, self-expression and communication skills. He was a professional actor and presenter for nearly 20 years – appeared in theatres all over the country, and became a familiar face on TV. A pioneer of using theatre techniques in education and subsequently business, he has written scripts for radio and TV (including *Not the Nine O'Clock News*) and created many training films. He is an acclaimed public speaker and regularly presents or runs sessions at large conferences throughout Europe. He works regularly with companies advising on people development issues, particularly around culture change and leadership.

Andrew Leigh and Michael Maynard run Maynard Leigh Associates, the management development and consultancy service. Many major organisations are MLA clients, including Vodafone, Aviva, Hewlett Packard, Campbells, The Stock Exchange and *Financial Times*.

For information about leadership skills training, Leading Your Team workshops leadership profile and leadership coaching at:

Maynard Leigh Associates
Marvic House
Bishops Road
London SW6 7AD
Tel: 020 7385 2588
email: inspiration@maynardleigh.co.uk
www.maynardleigh.co.uk

OTHER TITLES IN THE SERIES

PERFECT
LEADER

All you need to get it right first time

Andrew Leigh and
Michael Maynard

RANDOM HOUSE

BUSINESS BOOKS

This edition published by Random House Business Books in 2003

7 9 10 8 6

First published in the United Kingdom by Arrow Books in 1996.

Random House Business Books
The Random House Group Limited
20 Vauxhall Bridge Road, London, SW1V 2SA

Random House Australia (Pty) Limited
20 Alfred Street, Milsons Point, Sydney,
New South Wales 2061, Australia

Random House New Zealand Limited
18 Poland Road, Glenfield
Auckland 10, New Zealand

Random House South Africa (Pty) Limited
Isle of Houghton, Corner of Boundary Road & Carse O'Gowrie,
Houghton 2198, South Africa

Random House UK Limited Reg. No. 954009

www.randomhouse.co.uk

businessbooks@randomhouse.co.uk

A CIP catalogue record for this book
is available from the British Library

Papers used by Random House
are natural, recyclable products made from wood grown in
sustainable forests. The manufacturing processes conform to
the environmental regulations of the country of origin.

ISBN 9781844131471

Typeset in Sabon by SX Composing DTP, Rayleigh, Essex

Printed and bound in Great Britain by
CPI Antony Rowe, Chippenham, Wiltshire

Contents

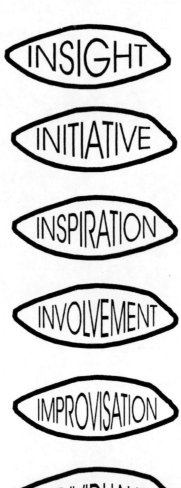

INSIGHT

INITIATIVE

INSPIRATION

INVOLVEMENT

IMPROVISATION

INDIVIDUALITY

IMPLEMENTATION

Introduction

Halfway through conducting a piece of music the conductor Andre Previn left the podium. Without this commanding figure the audience expected the orchestra to fall apart. Instead it played on beautifully, completing the piece with gusto.

Previn was making a point. If his role was not to dictate the players' every action, what on earth was it? He certainly was not there just to 'manage' the situation, or merely to keep time. His real rôle was to provide direction – the core purpose of leadership.

By now surely we know what it takes to be an effective leader? Not a bit of it! Despite endless research and leadership books stretching back beyond Machiavelli, there remains no consensus, on how to learn or hold on to leadership.

Here then is at least one reliable fact:

- We recognise leaders once they have performed certain actions. We tend to say with hindsight – 'that was leadership.'

So you can feel encouraged. We know leadership only when we experience it. Defining or describing it merely produces endless debates around meaning.

At it simplest, leadership is about achieving things with other people's support, which is why in *Perfect Leader* we tend to talk of supporters, rather than followers.

At its most complicated, leadership describes behaviour that only a rare few of us can expect to emulate. Between these two extremes is the reality:

- Leadership is a relationship between the person leading and those they lead

Perfect Leader is about your ability to build such a relationship and understand what helps create it.

REALITY CHECK

There seems no real connection between your depth of experience and your ultimate performance as a leader. Hugely experienced people may nevertheless be terrible leaders, while a new employee may demonstrate unexpected leadership from the start.

One of the most detailed investigations by Jim Collins in *Good To Great*, (Random House 2001), into highly successful organisations, has uncovered an important new picture of high-level leadership. These people tend to be a curious mixture.

- Modest yet wilful
- Humble yet fearless.

Unlike the 'me-centred' image we tend to hold of leaders in the public eye, the reality is that the most successful

2

business leaders are reluctant to talk about themselves. They are not exactly shrinking violets, it's just that their focus is on their relationship with others, not themselves.

Another critical finding about successful leaders is that their first priority, far from being to create 'a vision' or a 'destination' is the more prosaic one of getting the right people around them. That also means moving the wrong people out of the way.

Only when the high level leader has the right people 'on board the bus' does the attention shift to 'where shall we drive it?'

HOW PERFECT?

Is there any such thing as a *Perfect Leader* or even perfect leadership?

There are no perfect leaders, unless you count all the dead ones. Nor does being a leader make you suddenly perfect. Somehow even ineffective leaders may manage to survive.

What will it take for you to succeed? At least three important realisations will influence your chances:

• That leaders are made not born
• That you need others to be a leader
• That there is no need to be perfect

Leadership starts here! It does not matter whether you are already in a formal leadership role or not. People with no previous experience have often begun behaving like a leader and subsequently triumphed. Annually thousands of people learn and start practising the basics of leadership. You can do it too.

You can practice leadership anywhere – in a team, at home, in a Parent/Teachers Association, in a hobby group, in your family. Wherever there is a job to be done you can draw on your natural creative energy to start practicing leadership.

'If a man is called to be a street sweeper, he should sweep streets even as Michelangelo painted, or Beethoven composed music, or Shakespeare wrote poetry. He should sweep streets so well that all the hosts of heaven and earth will pause to say, here lived a great street sweeper, who did his job well.'
Martin Luther King

WHAT TYPE OF LEADERSHIP?

In our work in organisations we broadly identify two sorts of leadership:

- Enabling
- Inspirational

The first is mainly what managers do by supporting, facilitating and motivating those around them. This type of leadership is the opposite of command and control. It is about releasing people's potential and getting the best from them. It does not, for example, require much strategic thinking or other aspects of higher-level leadership.

'My generation has grown up in a world steeped in hierarchy. We are used to having control. Used to sitting at the top and setting direction with little resistance. That

is just not feasible anymore. Young people will not tolerate it. And neither will the marketplace, I have been working hard to define my own role, as a leader. I spent 30 years training for a job that no longer exists. I have had to adapt rapidly.'

Durk Jager – when Chairman and CEO of Proctor & Gamble

If you are already at the top of your organisation, you probably see the sense of personally adopting an enabling style, because you know that it generally gets results. However, it is ideally suited to middle and junior managers. *Their* type of leadership mainly focuses on operational issues, drawing the best performance from reports and from others not directly accountable to them.

Such leadership seldom relies on formal authority or hierarchical position. Instead it uses involvement, consultation, promoting creativity, sharing information and coaching. People receive guidance and stimulation to perform at their best. Leaders spend considerable time encouraging and enabling group behaviour. For example, virtual teams radically affect the team leader's role. With the members perhaps scattered across the globe and perhaps not even direct reports, the leader must rely entirely on a facilitating style that respects individual contributions.

INSPIRATIONAL

Inspirational leaders are special because, amongst their other many qualities, they know how to make contact with individuals.

Inspirational leadership once meant 'strong leadership' allied to powerful charisma. People expected leaders to impose their persona indelibly on the entire organisation. Robert Horton as CEO of BP did that and had many valuable personal qualities, yet he came across as arrogant and self-aggrandizing. So BP fired him.

We worked briefly with a well-known UK privately owned midlands brewery where the MD's personality was certainly stamped over the entire company. The trouble was he inspired fear, acted inconsistently and destroyed people's readiness to contribute or be creative.

Inspirational leaders are different. They inspire through a mixture of behaviours that cannot easily be reduced to a tidy set of rules. What we offer in *Perfect Leader* are practical guidelines to help you *perfect* your leadership, even if perhaps you never quite become perfect.

From our work with hundreds of teams and many leaders we find the Inspirational ones tend to be highly effective at the the 7 I's

- **Insight**
- **Initiative**
- **Inspiration**
- **Involvement**
- **Improvisation**
- **Individuality**
- **Implementation**

These have stood the test of time. Talk to any effective leader about how they do it and they soon start referring in some way to one or more of these 7 I's though not necessarily using the identical terminology.

The 7 I's are a useful way of remembering the basic principles of inspirational leadership. They also highlight perhaps the most powerful element of effective leadership:

- The ability to see what is needed

In working with leaders we often invite them to rate themselves against these areas of inspirational leadership. Next they ask some of their supporters to say how they experience their particular leadership. The answers are often surprising and sometimes not entirely comfortable.

Here for example is a 7 I's profile:

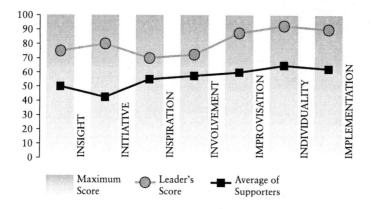

In this example the leader tended to self rate much higher than the scores given by the supporters.

Successful leaders share a common wish to develop themselves and this kind of information can be useful in identifying areas for change and selecting the priorities for personal development.

To conduct your own 7 I's leadership profile visit: http://www.maynardleigh.co.uk/inter_sect.shtml. This is a fee-based service.

CHARISMA

Even today when people talk about inspirational leadership, they still mainly mean charisma. We see it in the publicity-seeking individual leaders such as Virgin's Richard Branson, or in the endless adulation of powerful figures such as Lord Brown, BP's much praised CEO, or in the breathless appreciation of start up winners like the leaders of Lastminute.com.

What Jim Collins' (*Good to Great*) research has decisively confirmed is that charisma is seldom a decisive factor in what makes a truly effective and inspirational leader.

'Charisma becomes the undoing of leaders, making them inflexible and convinced of their own infallibility and unable to change.'
Peter Drucker

Being inspirational once meant that the leader alone did the inspiring, setting the agenda for everyone else's performance. New style inspirational leadership is more demanding.

Instead it promotes vision, is passionate about proclaiming and pursuing core values and provides uplifting examples of behaviour and communication to would-be supporters. Such leadership models the way so that others can follow.

SUPPORTERS

You are never a leader in isolation. It is not only what you do that counts, how you behave, what orders you give. It is also how others choose to respond to you. No wonder that the Chinese philosopher Lao-Tzu advised: 'To lead people, walk behind them.'

An actor on stage playing a king seems regal only because other actors are prepared to behave as *if* he is the king. No amount of regal posturing does the trick. Other people must react to the person as their leader. This applies equally to you.

Everyone, including you, is a potential leader, though not necessarily permanently. When you propose an idea at work, you are 'taking the lead' even if briefly. When you say 'I'll do that' in response to something that needs doing, you are also 'leading'.

Informal leadership based on behaviour, rather than relying on a formal role, moves around, in a group of people, particularly in highly creative situations where ideas and energy are rapidly shared. Nowadays, organisations are more aware of the value of informal leadership and many are trying hard to encourage it.

Since being a leader depends on others and is never in isolation, there are important ingredients making leadership possible:

The person . . . the situation . . . timing . . . other people

You can influence all of these to some extent.

People who make it possible for you to lead are sometimes described rather dismissively as 'followers'. This suggests passivity though, and underestimates how dependent you are on such people. They are more like supporters, or even constituents.

To lead, you do not need to be perfect. Our knack of idealising leaders arises from our natural way of compressing the so-called great ones into a single powerful quality: Nelson's strategy, Gandhi's persistence, Luther King's vision, Florence Nightingale's commitment, Pankhurst's determination, Churchill's oratory, Mandela's forgiveness, Mother Teresa's compassion.

Without such qualities perhaps you can never be a leader? History shows it to be otherwise. Even great leaders are flawed and less than perfect. Their skill is in getting things done despite their limitations, often in totally unexpected ways.

LIKEABILITY

An opinion poll on Moses would have shown that his vision and iron determination were hated by many of his flock, yet they still followed him into the desert and out the other side. So you do not need to be totally likeable to succeed as a leader. Few effective ones expect to be universally liked.

Indeed taking the lead may make you thoroughly unpopular. People such as Alan Sugar of Amstrad, or Rupert Murdoch the media baron, for example, are hardly popular figures, even amongst many of their staff. Yet they undoubtedly lead. However, they probably do so *despite* their abrasive personalities or style, rather than because of it. Whether as a leader it is better to be loved or feared has never been resolved.

INTEGRITY

Caesar Borgia reformed his country, restoring order and obedience. Hitler built nationwide roads and ended unemployment. Both despots were cruel, charismatic and failed to respect the difference between ends and means. Both ultimately failed.

Leadership can be regarded as amoral, it merely exists or it does not. However, leadership that does not contribute to human happiness, or that ultimately fails because of its destructive tendencies, is not the focus of *Perfect Leader.* We focus on leadership that contributes constructively to human happiness, earning wide respect, possessing integrity and also achieving business success.

You will need to discover your own unique way of leading. Merely copying other leaders and their personalities is unlikely to make you sufficiently special to gain real supporters. To discover your special leadership abilities means being willing to keep learning and growing as a human being:

The best leaders know themselves and what they want.

- Most leaders are made, not born
- You can learn to lead
- You are not a leader in isolation, there must be people willing to be led – supporters
- Leading means you may be respected, not necessarily liked
- You need to discover your own unique way of leading
- Leaders keep learning, growing, know themselves and what they want

PRACTICE

Few leaders always get it right first time. You learn to lead by continuously learning and adjusting to achieve your vision. Are you willing to keep learning and give yourself lots of practice? Only by trying things out will you discover what works for you as a leader. You can never assume that because another leader has adopted some way of getting things done, it will automatically work for you too.

Practice is how we learn most things and leadership is no different. Seek opportunities for practising your leadership in as many different settings as possible. Only through practice will you come to lead instinctively, taking the role effortlessly, almost without thinking.

'I believe we learn by practice. Whether it means to learn to dance by practising dancing or to learn to live by practising living, the principles are the same. In each, it is the performance of a dedicated precise set of acts, physical or intellectual, from which comes shape of achievement, a sense of one's being, a satisfaction of spirit. One becomes in some area an athlete of God.'
Martha Graham, dancer and teacher.

Practice is one of the most important ways you gain self-confidence as a leader. So, like a musician practising the scales, or an actor rehearsing lines, keep practising the 7 I's of leadership.

Leadership style
What kind of leadership style should you adopt? Maybe you should be a decisive, autocratic leader who brooks no opposition but gets amazing things done. Or perhaps you should be a quiet, consultative leader who never makes a move without fully involving everyone.

There is no 'should'. All leaders develop a personal style that is unique to them and you will have to do the same. However, certain trends are making it harder to be one kind of leader as opposed to another, and there is also some evidence that having only one style of leadership is too limiting. You need a whole repertoire of styles, which you may adopt for different circumstances.

The way organisations are moving for the foreseeable future suggests that the old style 'command and control' type leader is no longer so effective. This is because hierarchy is giving way to the idea of 'community' of shared interests and stakeholders.

New-style leadership is about facilitative, empowering relationships with those who might support a leader. In fact the relationship is mutually supportive, rather than dependent and subordinate. In productive work, effective leaders are not commanders and controllers, bosses and big shots. They are servers and supporters, partners and providers.

This newer form of leadership style unleashes much more:

- Energy
- Talent
- Commitment

CHAPTER 1

Insight

'Couldn't you see?' she yells, ready to storm out of the meeting.

'See what?' you say, hopelessly looking around.

'You must be blind, not to have noticed what's happening around here.'

Many of us have probably experienced missing the obvious. Remarks like 'it was staring you in the face' or 'you can't see the wood for the trees' may have accompanied these possibly humiliating moments. Sometimes it is only with hindsight that we realise the signs were there all the time.

Insight is your ability to accurately see events, circumstances and people, and be able to make sense of them. Inspirational leaders are particularly strong on insight. Although this can seem a mysterious quality, in essence most people can learn how to develop it.

Insight depends on using both sides of your brain, the logical part that loves to classify and analyse and the intuitive part that just 'knows'. Since we each tend to use one or either type of thinking at the expense of the other this can make our use of insight less effective.

For example, if you tend to be mainly a logical, systematic person you can begin improving your powers of

15

insight by deliberately tapping into the part of your brain that relies on instinct, feeling and emotion.

'You get your intuition back when you make space for it, when you stop the chattering of the rational mind.'
Anne Lamott, author

If you tend to rely heavily on your gut feeling and an intuitive sense of what to do next, you can also learn to take advantage of your brain's analytical powers. Even if you are mainly instinctive, your brain still has an extraordinary ability to classify and break down information into smaller, more manageable chunks.

Insight is essential for interpreting apparently disorganised information. It allows us to 'read' the environment and where necessary relate it to a plan of action.

People, events and circumstances often appear chaotic or meaningless.

For example, sometimes you perform at your best while at other times you feel sluggish. Why? Members of your team behave in a peculiar way. Why? A previously strong market position suddenly appears under threat. Why? Customers who once loved your service no longer seem enamored by it. Why? Faced with such uncertainty and disarray, many of us simply give up, regarding the world as hopelessly confusing. It is insight though that helps us make sense of these complexities.

This ability to interpret the world around and use insight involves:

- Self-awareness
- Understanding of others
- Seeing the situation

SELF-AWARENESS

Who am I, what impact do I have on people, how do I need to change?

Leadership is autobiographical. Who you are, is how you lead. The better you know yourself, the more confident you will be using your leadership capabilities. Leaders don't necessarily share their self-knowledge with anyone and many are undeniably lonely at the top. The astute ones though, want to know what is happening within them and how it affects their outward behaviour.

Self-awareness has received considerable attention from researchers, particularly from the work of Daniel Golman and his observations on emotional intelligence. It has fostered the growth of 360-degree feedback tools enabling leaders to test how they see themselves against the reality of how others experience them. (See the 7 I's profile on page 126)

Becoming self-aware is not nearly as mystical as it sounds. It is how you see yourself; understand your personality, its strengths and weaknesses and impact on others. Deliberately or otherwise, successful leaders develop considerable personal insight.

If you hate the idea of increasing your self-awareness or it makes you feel really uncomfortable, then perhaps you should reconsider whether you truly want to be a leader.

'You can't lead a cavalry charge if you think you look funny on a horse'
John Peers, President of Logical Machine Corporation

Genuine self-awareness comes gradually, rather than instantly, like switching on a light. Occasionally though, one might suddenly acquire an entirely new perspective on the world. Self-aware people:

- Keep looking at what they do and how they do it

Successful leaders know their leadership is always on the line, liable to vanish instantly. So either consciously or unconsciously, they constantly check how they are performing. It is rather like actors or musicians wanting to know what the director, conductor or critic thinks about their performance.

Self-aware people are not mere navel gazers. They simply make enough time to reflect, to occasionally pause and wonder what is going on inside them. This can be hard in a world that seems to work by sound bites, instant communication and pressure for results.

Self-awareness differs from being self-conscious. When you are highly self-conscious you can hardly absorb anything that is not solely about you, rather than others. This self obsession gets in the way of seeing what is happening around you.

Become more self-aware by consciously exploring:

- What is driving you
- Your current feelings
- Your present attitudes
- How others around you are feeling and reacting
- Your impact on people around you

Where would you get such feedback? Obviously you do not have it right now. You have to deliberately seek it. This means asking people, seeking their opinions and enquiring what they are thinking. You may need to put yourself in potentially uncomfortable situations, or be quite personally vulnerable to obtain the information you need.

For instance, you could tell some trusted colleagues that you are embarking on a personal project and would benefit from their opinion of how you come across in certain situations. Specify the areas, such as in meetings, or when meeting new customers. And encourage them to be truthful and not hold back. You would also benefit from seeking new experiences and seeing how you react to them. And by perhaps attending a conference or seminar, you can see how strangers react to you.

Checking it out

There are many ways of exploring yourself and who you are. The method matters less than being willing to uncover more about you. Many people though, shy away from such self-examination, in fact any type of introspection. But such people seldom make good leaders.

Try developing a clearer picture of your own strengths and weaknesses by creating a sort of personal balance sheet. Use this to explore how best to develop further and become a more complete person. Even writing down such a list is a useful start. You need never show it to anyone else.

Psychometric tests, or personality profiles, are also ways of gaining a new perspective on yourself. These may have many different purposes. For example, to clarify your preferred role in a team, your tendency to take instant action or time to reflect, whether you care more about people or things, whether you are introspective or an extrovert, how you prefer to learn and so on.

Self-aware people possess a natural curiosity about themselves. They keep pursuing questions such as:

- Why did I do that?
- What effect did I have?
- Why did that work?
- How could I do that better?
- What went wrong with what I did?
- That worked, how can I do it again?
- How did they react to what I said or did?
- How am I feeling right now?

Internal cast

Mature actors know that within themselves they have accumulated a vast array of 'people' allowing them to portray these externally. This internal cast of characters exhibits and expresses different aspects of themselves.

In working with business leaders to develop their self awareness, we regularly use this insightful model of an 'inner cast of characters'. For it is not only actors who possess this rich inner world; every human being does. We each have many different 'people' inside us: the achiever, the bully, the coward, the lover, the joker, the procrastinator, the doer, the enthusiast, the painter, the eccentric and so on. These influence how we behave and respond to the world. Some psychologists refer to them as sub-personalities.

Begin exploring your internal cast of characters by thinking how you tend to respond to different kinds of events in your life. See whether you can identify an internal character that seems to keep occurring:

- When does this aspect of yourself seem to take over?
- What appears to trigger this character's appearance?
- What control do you have over this character?
- What influence does this internal character have on your leadership?
- Does this character get in the way or help?

Becoming more self-aware involves learning to recognise and draw on these inner resources. For example, in certain situations even the most ruthless leaders can access their inner compassion. Or the Mr Nice Guys in the business world usually realise the importance of accessing the part of themselves that is decisive, challenging and confronting, because certain situations require it.

Expanding your leadership style through your different internal characters gives you more options, a larger repertoire. Styles though can have both a positive and negative effect on your own and other people's performance. Goleman for example highlights six core leadership styles only four of which have a constructive impact: authoritative, affinitive, democratic and coaching. The other two styles of being coercive and pace-setting usually have an adverse impact.

Knowing more about your preferred leadership style and your internal characters could really enhance your leadership insight.

Learning Events

Workshops and learning events that challenge your current perspective on the world and focus on how you are functioning as a person, can also help develop self-awareness.

There are many different self-development courses from which to choose. Some use a particular approach such as psychotherapy, psycho synthesis, transactional analysis, meditation or Neuro Linguistic Programming. Others are more eclectic, using a wide range of development techniques to broaden understanding.

Give yourself a target of attending at least one self-development course every six months. See it as an enjoyable challenge, rather than a burden. After all, if you are not interested in developing you, who else will be?

In summary, growing self-awareness comes from an ongoing process of investing in your own personal development.

UNDERSTANDING OTHERS

What do supporters need, why do they do what they do, how can they be helped to perform better?

Understanding others is not about being clairvoyant, though it can appear that way to those on the receiving end. For example, supporters say things like:

- 'How did she know I felt that way?'
- 'He said exactly what I was thinking too'
- 'She really got my point'

How do leaders achieve this effect on people? Broadly it comes down to really listening and understanding others using acute observation, along with natural powers of analysis and instinct.

It is a lifetime's work to build this ability to understand others, which is why successful leaders never abandon trying to grasp what drives their supporters. They keep enquiring, either openly by observing and asking the right questions or at some deeper level through natural instinct and developing a true 'feel' for the situation.

You can apply similar methods to gain more understanding of other people. Again, it is less the method you use that is important, than your willingness to harness your natural curiosity, your determination to discover more.

With a team for example, you might regularly ask

people to explain how they are feeling, what they are thinking, what concerns them. More formally, you could ask everyone to complete a series of question-naires that reveal their personal preferences and other information.

One of the best ways of really understanding others is through people watching – consciously observing them in all kinds of different situations, observing how they behave, rather than just taking their words and actions for granted. Do you know more about your computer than about those you lead?

Insight into people and their potential for outstand-ing performance starts with observation, and is fuelled by natural curiosity. Through intense observation, along with your other powers of analysis and instinct, you attempt to build up a picture of those around you.

Leaders who replace being judgmental with being curious, start to understand others better by giving some thought to others. You could focus on a colleague with whom you would like a better working relationship and ask yourself:

- Why do they do what they do?
- Why do they behave the way they do?
- What are their characteristic actions or speech?
- What are they feeling?
- What do they want?
- What isn't being said?
- How do their words differ from actions?
- What are these actions telling me?
- If I were that person how would I feel?
- How am I similar to them?
- How am I different to them?
- What motivates that person?
- What would be a challenge for them?

- What would that person really need?
- What would be a treat for them?
- What's going on in their life outside of work?
- How does this affect the way they behave?

You do not lead in a vacuum. You have to be constantly scanning for signals that suggest what to do next. Start becoming a kind of detective, using your curiosity and interest to make sense of what is needed. Try putting yourself mentally into your followers' shoes. How might they respond to different situations?

You can even do this physically. For example, to begin to understand body language for instance try and replicate a person's posture, gestures or expression. Privately imitate that person and see what it feels like to walk around and express yourself in the way that they do. You may acquire some really valuable clues about how they tick.

Best of all, ask them! People will often tell you what they need. By not asking them, you ignore an essential source of information.

Channels
Formal channels or even contact solely at work may not be enough to enhance your understanding of people. You may occasionally need to sacrifice valuable personal time to socialise in non work settings.

For example, Archie Norman, responsible for supermarket Asda's dramatic turnaround, held regular Monday night, five-aside football matches where people were more willing to relax and be forthcoming. Famous leaders have often abandoned their own security or prestige surroundings to hear directly from their supporters' own lips. Certain generals for instance, have even disguised themselves, mingling freely with their troops so as to hear for themselves what people are thinking and saying.

Similarly the founder of Wal Mart in America regularly arrived at selected stores around six or seven in the morning. That way he could meet employees arriving for work and spend time talking to them before they got too involved with their duties. In the UK Tesco expects all its managers to spend at least a week a year out in the stores doing basic jobs such as stacking shelves or working in the stock room.

Even when you think you have gained a clear picture of what other people are thinking, feeling or saying, you may still need to check it for accuracy. This means testing your conclusions by asking whether your view of what they think and feel is correct. Start conversations with some provocative question, for example, 'I was wondering how you felt about the current changes?' or 'You seem to be a bit quiet today, is there anything going on?'

As long as such questions are asked in an unthreatening way, you may well unearth crucial information that will help avoid unmotivated behaviour and wasted effort.

In summary, understanding others is a continuous process of:

- Observing
- Exploring
- Testing

PERCEPTIONS OF SITUATIONS

What is really happening – in the office, in the company, in the market place, in the industry, with the competition, in the future? What needs to happen next?

We each view the world through our own mental maze, established over many years. Because of our different experiences, no two people ever see the world identically. Inspirational leaders though, show an acute grasp of reality, even setting outrageous goals and sharing seemingly impossible visions. What looks like a forlorn hope to one person, becomes a *raison d'être* to an inspirational leader.

Inspirational leaders see things as they really are or differently to other people. Their reality is not necessarily more objective or accurate, only more strongly held. Powerful leaders enable others to see the world through their eyes.

When an effective leader says 'this is the situation', we may not necessarily agree, yet we respond because in some way it makes sense to us. For example, most people simply accepted that the increasing crime rate in New York City was irreversible. However, James Wilson and George Kelling came up with what became known as the 'broken windows' theory. They believed that by constantly repairing the windows and painting over the graffiti on the subway, they would create a symbol of regeneration. This new way of looking at the situation, plus a mass of other apparently minor initiatives resulted in the dramatic decline in the crime rate.

How do leaders arrive at a different reality from the rest of us? It partly arises from being willing to adopt new or discard old: views, prejudices, assumptions, beliefs, and interpretations.

They also view the world differently by constantly using their senses to 'see' what each situation requires. These 'senses' include:

- A sense of humour
- A sense of wonder
- A sense of occasion
- A sense of danger
- Common sense

A sense of humour
Leaders with a great sense of humour seldom constantly crack jokes, rather the opposite. Instead they use their humour sensitively and appropriately. Generally, it is best leaving jokes to comedians who take years mastering their craft.

What exactly is a good sense of humour? It is mainly keeping things in perspective, debunking pomposity or reducing complexity to a simple observation. People facing the direst situations will often focus on something amusing.

For example, Iranian hostages Brian Keenan and John McCarthy used humour to get them through years in the most awful conditions. So too did Nelson Mandela during his time on Robben Island. Some people recall the Second World War years not just for the 'Dunkirk spirit' but also for how people both laughed, and cried together.

A sense of wonder
All people need 'wondering time'. It can be some of the most valuable time you spend as a leader.

A report from the Roffey Park Management Institute on how directors think, found that their best ideas occur away from the workplace – commonly on their own and in relaxed settings, such as on train or plane journeys, walking the dog, or on the beach. They stressed the importance of 'reflective time' as a route to insight and foresight:

- Leaders sometimes apply their natural sense of wonder to solve problems. Bill Bowerman, the inventor of Nike shoes for example, wondered what would happen if he put rubber into his waffle iron.

- Fred Smith, founder of Federal Express wondered why there couldn't be a reliable overnight mailservice. Masaru Ibuka, honorary chairman of Sony, wondered what would happen if they removed the recording function and speakers and put headphones in the recorder, thus creating the Walkman.

- The inventor of Freeplay, the clockwork radio, wondered why poor people in under developed countries had to keep buying expensive batteries to power the sound. Such wondering is highly valuable, and frequently interpreted as foresight.

- James Dyson wondered why vacuum cleaners never really seemed to improve, lost their suction and had endless replacement bags.

Try a bit of wondering as part of your daily leadership routine! For example, try wondering:

- How can we stay ahead of the game?
- What new developments are over the horizon?
- What unexpected situations might we plan for?
- What if current trends were reversed?

A sense of occasion

Inspirational leaders know the value of encouraging a sense of occasion. It can take true leadership to say in effect 'Hey! Let's just stop a moment and savour what's happened.' Such leaders constantly seek these opportunities or keep inventing them.

Even if you are not a party animal there is usually someone around who certainly is. Find those people and invite them to help the company celebrate regularly, they will often jump at the chance.

The leadership skill is creating a culture where everyone feels free to suggest a reason to celebrate and make it happen. It is through their sense of occasion that leaders ensure that people around them take time to notice that something special is happening, and deserves being honoured – whether it be an anniversary of someone's tenure in the organisation or a successful deal.

A sense of danger

'Only the paranoid survive,' claimed Intel's Andy Grove memorably, and in some ways he is right. Leaders who want outstanding individual company or individual performance need to tap into their own natural and primitive sense of danger to sense what might be going wrong.

This sensing and anticipating often sets the insightful leader apart. Bill Gates with his 'we're never more than two years away from disaster' clearly lives a daily nightmare that unless he and his company stay fully alert it may not survive. That he nearly missed the relevance of the Internet is well known. Equally important though, was his rapid response once he sensed the danger, re-orientating the entire company in a new direction in weeks, rather than months or years.

Common Sense

'I'm absolutely staggered, myself at what has happened. But I am surprised that other people are amazed at what we have done at Carphone Warehouse because it's not particularly amazing. It's all applied common sense, what we do.'

Charles Dunstone, chairman and majority shareholder of Carphone Warehouse.

Leaders who want to create outstanding performance naturally look for solutions. Yet the amount of material and advice on offer makes the task seem impossibly complicated. Inspirational leaders use common sense to cut through complexity to arrive at an elegant simplicity. Such leaders are willing to trust their own common sense, arguing for example 'let's throw out the rule book', 'to hell with how it's always been done', 'this feels right to me.'

Tapping into one's natural senses may be discomforting yet also productive. Sooner or later and often sooner, the universe comes knocking with a fresh dose of reality. Confronting what is happening around you is one of the best ways of using your insight.

Looking for alternatives, seeking examples that seemingly contradict current organisational culture, seeing where the rules are being broken productively, may all help your ability to see what is not yet manifest. Ask colleagues questions such as:

- What are you working on that's new or different?
- If we had a magic wand, how could we transform things around here?
- How could we make things ten times better around here?

Just as it is useful to put yourself in others' shoes and see it from their point of view, so it helps if you can stand outside a situation, seeing it from afar. This allows you to grasp the bigger picture, preventing you from becoming buried in detail. This wider perspective prompts you to see where things are going, or how they are developing, rather than being stuck in the current situation.

Practice
Everything to do with leadership insight takes practice. Certainly some people may have been born more intuitive than others. Yet you can develop your insight. by practicing observation, trying to understand other people, attempting to see reality and imagining the future.

Spend some time each day just looking. Value this time as essential to the business. In these periods of reflection you may well gain an insight that could save or make your organisation huge profits – far more than the day-to-day slog of repetitive activities. That's what leaders contribute.

'To practice means to perform in the face of obstacles, some act of vision, of faith, of desire. Practice is a means of inviting the perfection desired.'
Martha Graham, dancer and teacher

CHAPTER 2

Initiative

'I am certainly not one of those who need to be prodded. In fact if anything I am a prod.'
Winston Churchill

When a new chairman of Shell took over he reviewed the initiatives of his many predecessors. Without exception they too had conducted reviews followed by announcements of major new programmes of change.

Yet his research revealed that virtually none of these initiatives had taken hold. What he was confronting was the raw truth that in large, complex organisations, those at the top can easily become marooned in their offices, bombarded with letters, emails and voice mails, visitors, and meetings. Just reading could fill the entire time. In fact one need never implement anything of substance and simply be reactive.

Inspirational leaders are people who make things happen, they take initiative and persuade others to join their cause. You can exercise these skills anywhere, inside a company, a voluntary organisation, a public agency, within a team or on the shop floor. You do not need to start your own business or command a major institution.

Use initiative by taking:

- Responsibility
- Risks
- Direct action

Another clear sign that you are someone who initiates is your:

- Vitality

RESPONSIBILITY

'*A chief is a man who assumes responsibility. He says, "I was beaten" he does not say "my men were beaten."*'
Antoine de Saint-Exupury

You can usually spot someone showing leadership by whether they seem ready to take responsibility. People with leadership potential put themselves forward, or they accept a role when asked by others who turn to them for help.

Look for opportunities to take responsibility through:

volunteering; participating; being accountable; taking centre stage

Volunteering – is when you keep saying 'Yes' whenever a job needs doing, or a problem needs someone to solve it. Leaders willingly take things on, often the worst jobs or the ones with least apparent kudos. The act of putting themselves forward demonstrates leadership.

For example, when you say 'Yes I'll do that' you set

an example for others. You are indicating 'this is how it should be around here'. By volunteering you model how you believe others should perform, and inspire them to take responsibility too.

Volunteering also provides opportunities to learn and grow. You open yourself to new experiences and to change. Sometimes you do not know what you are letting yourself in for. Non leaders play it safe and avoid such risks.

There is always the danger of overdoing it, taking on excessive work. This is destructive. Only you can judge whether you can handle more, or are heading for burnout. Avoiding opportunities and playing safe though, stops you having personal challenges that help realise your own potential.

Participating – another test of your leadership potential is whether you take part in other people's projects. Your willingness to join a task force, a project group, a committee, a team activity, is an important sign of leadership in an organisation.

It is active, not passive, participation that builds leadership. Merely going along with the crowd is compliance. Active participation is demonstrating by your actions and behaviour that 'I want to contribute.'

Being accountable – shows you can be relied upon. First you make statements such as:

'I'll see that gets done'
'Leave that to me'
'That was my fault'
'I'll solve that'
'I got that wrong'
'I'll complete that on time'
'Nobody else is handling this, so I will'
'I'll take responsibility for that'

These are not empty words or phrases. Secondly, you need to gain a reputation for following through, backing up promises with actions that support them.

Inspirational leaders who take responsibility for their actions are willing to be vulnerable to criticism, questioning, sharing their own feelings. Far from making them look weak, such vulnerability makes them appear strong.

For example, in late 1999 Ford UK was accused of racism and harassment. Flying into the country to try and defuse the issue, the company's world chief executive Jaques Nasser, to the embarrassment of the UK management, held a 20-minute private meeting with an employee whom the company admitted had suffered repeated racist bullying. Further, he appointed an outsider from the company's continental operation to supervise the UK company's diversity programme. The impact on the unions was electric 'we have secured all we wanted'. Clearly Nasser took responsibility for what had gone wrong, and made himself accountable for change.

When you act as a leader people tend to say 'She does what she says she'll do' or 'You can rely on him to do that.' By showing that you are willing to stand up and be counted you put your personal values on public display.

When a serious mistake occurs don't try to pass the buck to someone else. Instead, be willing to shoulder some or all of the blame. People will tend to see you as willing to accept criticism as well as praise. Accountability could even be taking the blame for something that is not your fault. For example, if someone responsible to you makes a serious error, as a leader you cannot hide behind them and say 'I didn't do it.' To some degree you too are in the firing line.

Unlike managers, leaders never justify what they do solely by referring to rules, company policy, job descriptions, written briefs and other ways of denying responsibility.

Taking centre stage – is another aspect of taking responsibility. You allow your leadership to be seen and acknowledged. Although some leaders can be self-effacing, ultimately all are willing to stand in the limelight of their followers' attention.

Leaders we admire tend not to place themselves at the centre; instead placing others there. They do not seek attention so much as give it to others. However, they are prepared to be in the limelight when necessary. Occasionally the limelight is more intense, when events bring you into the public eye and attract the attention of the media. Leading means being prepared to be visible in whatever form this takes. You cannot both lead and remain a shrinking violet.

RISK

Leaders often extol the virtues of risk-taking to their supporters and then ruin it all by behaviour that in effect punishes any attempt at doing just that. Fear usually lies behind an inability to take risks:

- Fear of failure
- Fear of losing control
- Fear of criticism

Inspirational leaders invariably grasp the difference between being risky and being reckless.

Taking risks is simply part of the creative aspect of leadership that you need to become comfortable with and learn to handle. Avoiding being reckless is about unacceptably high consequences from some action.

For example Marconi fell from grace mainly because its leader recklessly embraced the telecommunications market while discarding the company's previous core strengths. In the case of Boo.com the founders hurtled from merely being risky in building their new business, to being reckless in burning through incredible sums of money until it simply ran out. Similarly, when the UK's boss of Alta Vista announced free access to the Internet, it emerged later that he had not consulted anyone, let alone his superiors in the States.

In contrast, Easy Jet's Chief Executive while certainly taking a large and costly risk in buying up the competing Go Airline, was not recklessly placing his entire company in jeopardy.

The more inspirational the leader, the more they seem willing to push the boundaries of risk towards what others may rightly or wrongly come to regard as recklessness. It can therefore be quite uncomfortable since you need to:

- Step out of your comfort zone
- Be non-compliant
- Handle rejection, disagreement and failure

Leaders willing to take risks can be inspiring to those around them, particularly when also placing their reputation or wealth on the line. James Dyson built a world-class company that overtook Hoover by taking informed risks that enabled him to overcome constant setbacks. When for example, Phillips Plastics held him to ransom on the cost of assembling his innovative cleaner he refused to be intimidated, daring to set up alternative facilities elsewhere, much to their amazement. His persistence, initiative and risk taking continue to attract a talented team of young designers around him.

Eric Schmidt who turned around the fortunes of Novell was unafraid to take risks to change the company's performance. 'You know it's a natural reaction to turn cautious when your company's in trouble,' he says 'but that's precisely the wrong tack to take. You have to give people freedom to pursue their passions. That's the only way to keep them focused and inspired and to ensure that you'll have a flow of new products to regain, retain or grow ground in the market.'

Stepping out of your comfort zone – happens by attempting something unfamiliar, where you are unsure about the outcome. It is when you:

- Disagree
- Say things that may upset people
- Do things that attract disapproval
- Break the rules
- Challenge convention
- Try new things
- Do what is right, rather than what is expected
- Question received wisdom
- Act without always knowing all the likely outcomes
- Deliberately put yourself in a learning situation
- Seek information on how others see you
- Commit to action without knowing if others will follow

Your comfort zone is the area of experience where you know what to expect and how you are likely to perform. While it may be a congenial place, it is also a limiting one. It shuts you off from all sorts of experiences, feedback and situations that might help you grow and develop as a person and as a leader.

Leaving your comfort zone involves new situations

where you do not know the rules or are unsure of how you will fare. Try giving yourself some systematic practice at this. For example, list twenty challenging things you would like to do, yet have never done before. These risks might be:

- **physical,** such as riding in a hot-air balloon, bungee jumping or being a blood donor
- **social,** such as attending an unusual sporting occasion, helping disabled kids, organising a street party
- **emotional,** such as confronting somebody with a difficult truth or expressing honest feelings to a person
- **political,** such as phoning a talk-radio show, making a speech, supporting a local campaign

Or breaking a habit, or presenting yourself in an unusual way etc.

Can you think of some activities that would develop you and make you feel stretched and challenged? They may be slightly daunting or merely involve doing something you have often delayed.

Choose twelve such challenging experiences and complete one each month, for a year. By the end of it you will have had an extraordinary time, while also growing and developing in important new ways.

Can't think of twelve such activities? Then it is time to get some fresh stimulus from talking to colleagues, going on a course, or whatever it will take to start the ball rolling.

Yet another way of exploring your present comfort zone is to begin deliberately breaking old patterns and habits. These are not necessarily wrong, but may merely stop you seeing the world afresh, limiting your vision and no longer providing stimulus.

For example, do you always take the same route home every day? Try three different ways and notice what you learn or how it stimulates you. If you always read one type of newspaper, drink one brand of lager, get up the same time most days, experiment with doing it differently for a month. If you always tend to work late, try having a whole week in which you go home early.

List some of your more obvious patterns or habits. You may need someone else close to you to help you spot some of these. Having identified half a dozen, find ways to break them and see how you feel. If even thinking about doing so makes you uncomfortable, it could be a good reason for taking action.

Challenging your own habits and patterns makes you more open to other people, to hearing what they have to say, to learning what they want. Besides, it stops you merely going through life on auto-pilot. For example, when senior managers in supermarkets occasionally stack shelves it always gives them new perspectives.

Non-compliance – is the need to assert yourself. Being unassertive is failing to say what you think and feel, or not attempting to do what you want. By contrast leaders continuously express what they want and communicate it, until they are heard.

While sometimes it's sensible to conform, there may be more occasions when you should really listen to your own impulses to act and express yourself strongly. Do you tend to sit on these impulses, saying nothing?

Leadership is speaking your truth, even when others may strongly disagree. It is being able to say 'no' to the crowd, doing what you think is right, even if it means being different.

Generally, managers do things right or 'correctly' by following the rules. Leaders, though, take the risk of deciding for themselves what is right and do it, often regardless of any rules or the expectations of others.

When the leaders of the Boeing company launched the famous 707 airliner, it was an enormous risk that could have sunk the entire company. Conventional management thinking would almost certainly have rejected it. Yet with hindsight it was entirely the right leadership choice.

How you handle rejection, disagreement and failure is another way of taking the initiative. Few people succeed in life without some setbacks, or finding that some people disagree with them. Leaders are ready to risk the experience of people failing to support them.

Unless you ask people to do something you may never know whether they will follow your wishes. Should they refuse or fail to commit themselves wholeheartedly, you may feel abandoned, betrayed or ignored. How do leaders cope with these negative experiences?

Effective leaders never allow setbacks to dent their self-confidence or to stop them heading in the direction they want to go. Faced with setbacks they are noticeably resilient. It is often in adversity that true leadership emerges. As the ancient saying goes: any fool can steer the ship when the sea is calm.

Try exploring how you handle rejection and disagreement. When was the last time things didn't go your way? Do you allow your reactions to undermine your leadership confidence?

Fostering your own and others' self-confidence is not just about being positive. When you communicate your belief that you will succeed or that your supporters can be successful you help them to extend themselves and to persevere.

'Only he can command who has the courage and initiative to disobey.'
William McDougal, psychologist

The best leaders keep their morale up in the face of rejection or failure by:

- Persistence
- Not personalising
- Re-framing

Effective leaders never seem to give up, pursuing their particular vision, long after others have fallen by the wayside. *Persistence* has its own re-enforcing effect on emotions. Sheer determination can drown out the siren voices of negativity. When you are persistent despite obstacles and setbacks, you start to become inspirational.

Excessive persistence, though, can become obduracy and be unhelpful. If you keep ignoring the reality around you, blindly continuing against all the evidence, you risk rejection. Mrs Thatcher's refusal to budge over the Poll Tax for example, almost certainly helped lose her the party's leadership.

Not personalising your setbacks is another key to dealing with rejection. Because you will face many setbacks in your leadership, it is important not to treat them as aimed at you personally. Often they are merely the result of forces beyond your immediate control. Try talking to an uninvolved person to gain a fresh perspective when your leadership seems to be meeting problems. Even leaders need mentors sometimes.

Re-framing is yet another way of dealing with setbacks and disagreements. Here you take a situation and restate it in new ways. For example, suppose you suggest that your company's computer system needs updating because it is now out of date and slow. If this proposal is rejected, rather than abandon it, you might start to reframe the issue as a need for better communications and ways of keeping in touch with customers. From this might eventually flow a greater readiness to consider a new system.

ADD VALUE

It was a Japanese leader who once commented 'I don't pay people to come to work; I pay them to "add value" to the business'. Inspirational leaders who show initiative do so partly through constantly adding value to their organisations.

This might be through their decisions, contacts, knowledge, experience, relationships and so on. But where once just a few leaders might have shouldered the burden of adding value, now companies are too complex and fast moving for such a narrow reliance.

The continued high turnover in CEOs around the world provides clear evidence that people now constantly want evidence that their leaders really are adding value and also know how to handle the creativity of others who want to add value too. High performing leaders create a culture that welcomes, collects and applies these contributions.

VITALITY

We expect our leaders to exhibit signs of vitality and it's a shock when they don't.

For example, though widely portrayed as visionary,

Bill Gates can be mercurial with wildly fluctuating energy levels and sudden lack of vitality. During his videotaped deposition in the US government's civil suit against Microsoft he acted bored or lost in thought, rarely looking up at his off-camera interlocutor. Was this really one of the most powerful business leaders in the world?

The next day's *New York Times* captured the shock experienced in the court room when it called him 'evasive and uninformed, pedantic and taciturn.' Though leadership vitality is a natural quality of every human being, it has to be resilient under tough or unpleasant circumstances.

Meet any effective leader and you are almost always struck by their vitality. This is only partly a natural gift. It is also a result of using their energy, to stay wide-awake, be constantly alert and naturally curious.

Vitality is hard to define precisely although, like leadership itself, you certainly know it when you see it.

'I think enthusiasm rubs off on people, like pollen on bees.'
Sir Terence Conran

You cannot expect to have vitality unless you are healthy, which means paying attention to the needs of your:

- Body
- Mind
- Spirit

Busy people often neglect exercise, without realising its contribution to their leadership potential. Regular exercise does more than keep in trim your muscles and other organs. It's like air-conditioning for the brain. It blows away the mental cobwebs and contributes to your state of alertness.

Managers often pay lip-service to maintaining a balance between work and non-work. Effective leaders, though, know it's essential for retaining their natural vitality. Richard Branson's balloon escapades and Ted Turner's boating exploits may have had publicity gains; less obviously they helped them to maintain and enhance their enjoyment of life and hence their natural vitality.

Leisure and holidays are essential for sustaining leadership energy. It is all too easy to burn out from work. The very word recreation is about re-creating your vitality. The best leaders realise that they need to take care of themselves to minimise the impact of stress.

Work often expresses who we are. Leaders create the work they want, rather than react to what is thrown at them. Being aware of the bigger picture of one's life is another powerful way of staying sane.

'One of the symptoms of an approaching nervous break-down is the belief that one's work is terribly important.'
Bertrand Russell

Vitality also stems from being open to *personal growth and learning*. To realise your full potential as a leader you must discover as much about yourself as possible, both your strengths and your own development needs.

Gaining the support of others is another important source of vitality. People love to be asked for their help. You can only create supporters by making room for people's contribution.

Being willing to say 'I don't know', is also a sign of strength, rather than weakness, as long as it's not a constant theme in your conversations. Allow yourself to be nurtured by others around you. To lead you do not need to be omnipotent.

CHAPTER 3

Inspiration

To inspire others first inspire yourself. There are conflicting views though on how leaders can best do that. One view is that inspiration stems from sheer hard work in a focused area, in which you are passionately interested.

The other source of inspiration is more eclectic. The HR director of Lloyds of London for example, seeks it in his bath, while the chairman of Mazda searches for it using Zen philosophy. The findings of 'Where do Directors get their Ideas from?' by Roffey Park Management Institute in the late 1990s suggested that 'ideas and insights tend to come to us away from work, because this is when we allow our minds to drift and dream.'

Leaders inspire, managers motivate. It is perfectly possible to survive as a manager without ever inspiring anyone. However you cannot be a leader without an ability to inspire. There may be plenty of motivating going on such as offering encouragement, setting goals and so on. Yet inspiring people is not motivation under another name. It alters people inwardly so that they think and act differently, often performing beyond their own and other's people's expectations.

So what exactly what is inspiration? In essence it's a

feeling, an experience, we are moved in some way. Consequently people now feel different and are willing to do unusual things: go beyond their present limits, show courage, deal with formidable odds, cope with impossible circumstances.

Often the most basic experiences can be unbelievably inspiring, such as a daily sunset or the birth of a child. In business, inspiration usually emerges as enabling people to perform beyond their normal limits, to go that extra mile, produce outstanding results and look forward to coming to work.

'And then there is inspiration. Where does it come from? Mostly from the excitement of living. I get it from the diversity of a tree or the ripple of the sea, a bit of poetry, the sighting of a dolphin breaking the still water and moving toward me . . . anything that quickens you to the instant.'
Martha Graham, dancer and teacher

Managers tend to see motivation as something *done* to people. True leaders, though, are more concerned with: awakening, stimulus, spirit, energy, zeal, enthusiasm, vigour, gusto, ebullience, sparkle. These are what make people support a leader.

Traditionally we associate inspiration as the preserve of artists or charismatic personalities. Yet when anyone has a good idea or feels strongly about something they can be inspiring to other people. When someone is inspired it is as if they have received a spark of genius from some other world. Such moments may appear to be totally fortuitous, but often they come as a result of a period of intense work.

'Inspiration is a guest who doesn't like to visit lazy people.'
Tchaikovsky

Although Tchaikovsky implies that it is hard work that leads to inspiration we suggest that how you work is equally important. Working smarter not harder may be the way to gain inspiration.

You can learn to inspire other people, not once but often. The inescapable starting point is:

To inspire others, first inspire yourself

Discovering what inspires you is always the first step to having an effect on other people. Making this discovery means you need to:

- Immerse yourself in what seems to get you excited, moves you, makes you feel uplifted
- Be willing to explore what inspires others
- Start making a list of events, poems, works of art, films, books, people, plays, scenery or whatever, that inspires you
- Start distinguishing between the mediocre and the inspirational

Leaders work hard at inspiration and know that it doesn't always come easy. Make a choice to spend as much time as you can with whatever it is that, for you, rises above the mundane.

When you are inspired you are passionate, persuasive, unselfconscious and a great communicator. Everyone has that potential, leaders just do it more often. Although one cannot reduce it to a simple formula the commonest elements are:

- Vision
- Communication
- Passion
- Trust

VISION

'The single defining quality of leaders is the capacity to create and realise a vision.'
Warren Bennis, US leadership expert

All leaders create a compelling vision, one that promises to take their supporters to a new place. Then they show how to turn that vision into a reality. You do not need to be unusually prescient, it is more to do with defining what you want the future to look like.

President George Bush complained he lacked 'the vision thing' while a newly appointed head of IBM, whose job was to rescue the ailing giant, said, 'the last thing IBM needs is a vision.' Both failed to realise that vision was not a vague dream of the future, but an intensely clear idea of what they wanted the future to look like.

Sometimes we resist working with vision because we think it is the privilege of only gifted people. However, if you have ever walked into a run-down flat or house and had an idea of how it could look, you are in the realm of vision. Being able to imagine it decorated and furnished, is a good start.

Similarly you create a picture for yourself of how your office could ideally function, or your team might perform brilliantly together, or your organisation thrive.

'I dream for a living.'
Steven Spielberg

Where does vision come from? It would be wonderful to wake one morning with a compelling one and doubtless some exceptional leaders do work that way. But it is a left-over myth from the era of command and control that it is entirely down to the leader to generate a clear picture of the future. This is increasingly unrealistic when many people hold knowledge and wisdom, and it is no longer confined to the top echelons.

'Our most important strategic decision was made not in response to some clear sighted corporate vision, but by the marketing and investment decisions of front line managers who really knew what was going on. We need to soften the strategic focus at the top so we can generate new possibilities from within the organisation.'
Andy Grove, Intel

Your supporters can help you

- identify the vision
- expand the vision
- translate it into a universal message

For example, Federal Express's famous three-word vision is People, Service, Profit. This apparently simple three-word picture of what drives the company took a considerable time and much mutual help to evolve.

Vision can be at three distinct levels:

- Strategic
- Tactical
- Personal

Strategic vision is the organisation's over riding philosophy and provides the framework into which all activities fit. Somebody has to hold this vision, never losing sight of it. This might be chief executive or the top management team. Ideally it is shared by everyone.

Tactical vision is the philosophy in action and provides people with clear methods for taking action. Often tactical vision comes down to a picture of how the strategic vision will be achieved. For example, 'To value quality above all else'.

Personal vision is each person's view of themselves as they would like to be – behaving so as to realise the vision.

Another way of tapping into your own vision is by exploring your own values. These are your core beliefs that you do not easily alter. Begin to unravel them by examining:

- What really matters to me in myself (eg. integrity, fun, action)
- What really matter to me in other people (eg frankness, fairness, timeliness)
- What material things really matter to me (eg car, house, salary)
- What intangibles really mater to me (eg environment, peace, excitement, sociability)

It is through clarifying these that you being to define what kind of future you want.

'[Visions] are like dreams, only they occur in the waking state.'
Carl. G. Jung

Many managers who aspire to be leaders complain that they cannot communicate a vision to their people because the organisation or the top team does not have one. They conclude they cannot have one either. Further, they feel the rapid changes in the market place makes it impossible to foresee where the company is going. This is a narrow view of what vision offers. Leaders can have a vision for how they run their part of the operation for instance. They can certainly have a picture of how life could be for those they lead. All visions operate within practical constraints. It's like saying, because I can't determine how the world will look in the future, I can't picture how my home can be improved.

Yet there is nothing more real than a compelling vision. People 'see' what could be, and are prepared to do extraordinary things to realise it.

'When a vision begins to form everything changes, including the air around me'
Jean Dixon in *Ruth Montgomery, A Gift of Prophesy*

As part of firming up their vision, inspirational leaders usually draw on a strong set of personal values that they willingly share with others. Their readiness to share these provides a compass, for both themselves and others to use.

Body Shop, *Prêt à Manger* and Ikea, are not just clear brands, they express the respective leaders' set of values and are strongly manifested in the business. When a director of RHM Foods was asked how it would survive huge changes in the industry he replied: 'It's our values that will see us through'.

COMMUNICATION

A vision that stays locked inside your head is useless. If you really care about your vision you will *want* to share it with others. It will inspire and excite you to the point where you cannot help telling other people about it.

Most effective managers are good communicators and leaders are even better at it. You do not need to persuade a leader that presentation matters, or that their message needs to have impact. They are already convinced. You may well need to refine your communication skills if you are to lead successfully. You can do this in several ways:

- Think visually
- Use specific, practical examples
- Keep your messages short
- Explain the likely results of what you want
- Show personal commitment
- Ceaselessly talk about your vision
- Listen carefully
- Practice new ways of explaining your leadership message

Thinking visually means developing ways of conveying your vision to build pictures in people's minds. Strive to create an image of what you want, an almost tangible visualization of how the future should look. This requires practice. Start by thinking of images that already strike you as powerful, whether these are advertising pictures, paintings, a scene from a film or a photograph from a book.

Using images gives practice to the part of the brain that works by instinct, feeling and non-verbal concepts. You can also use metaphors as ideas that convey what you want. For example, by imagining your growing company as yeast fermenting you are using a metaphor to express a vision.

What image would summarise the future you want to create? Finding a powerful image or interesting metaphor to describe it helps other people 'see' what you are seeking. Martin Luther King's famous 'I have a dream' speech is a perfect example of using image to encapsulate a vision.

Use specific, practical examples to bring your vision to life. People understand messages best through real instances to which they can personally relate. For instance, by telling people how they will be affected by what you want to do, you begin turning vision into a reality.

Keep your messages short to avoid clogging the communication channels. This is not the same as being a speaker of few words. Effective leaders realise that at any one moment people can only absorb a certain amount of information, and they become expert at reducing their communications to extremely simple ideas.

Explain the likely results of what you want. People need to understand how they will be affected by what you want to achieve. Use examples to bring these results to life. Suppose a company's vision is that it should be the customer's first choice, this might start to be translated into practical tasks such as always ensuring that the phone is answered within three rings.

Show personal commitment to what you want to achieve. This can be summed up as sharing your feelings with supporters. If you do not care, why should they? (See below, Passion.) Model the required behaviour. For example, if you wish to sponsor excellent customer care, then start by caring for your staff in an exceptional way.

Ceaselessly talk about your vision to others. Leaders persistently talk about what they want, what matters, what the vision is all about. To get your message across requires constant communication. This does not mean being a loud-mouthed bore. Just keep watching for any opportunity to share your ideals.

Listen carefully to what others have to say about your vision. This will help you to refine it. Communication is two-way and merely banging on about your idea stops you receiving invaluable input. Let people play devil's advocate with your idea. It will help you to clarify it and make you even more able to communicate it effectively.

PASSION

Call it passion, commitment or conviction. Whatever the name, powerful leaders have it in large measure. They also insist on sharing it, constantly.

Listen for example to Julian Richer talking about selling at his hi fi chain Richer Sounds, or James Dyson enthusing about his unique solution to vacuum cleaners, or Nick Park of *Wallace and Grommit* fame, on the potential of plasticine in animation, or Warren Buffet on entrepreneurial energy or Dianne Thompson on her Camelot staff and the lottery, or Michael Eisner on creativity at Disney. These people are hungry to share their picture of the future, to create an organisation permeated by passion.

Nor is their passion directionless. It is sharply focused around what they want to achieve. It is concentrated like a laser beam, slicing through objections, obstacles and negativity. It is hard to say no to someone who cares so strongly about something and difficult to resist being drawn into their vision and becoming engaged.

In business it is now more acceptable to talk of commitment or conviction than a decade ago. Effective leaders soon learn that it is passion that moves people to support them, not appeals to logic or a recital of facts and figures.

When Igor Andronov for example talked of the challenge ahead of him as the new head of one of the largest IT operations in Europe, after the merger of Lloyds and TSB banks, he did not feature the technical issues at all. Instead, he remarked that what he wanted his people to show was passion.

For anyone wanting to be an effective leader, the good news is that when you have found your passion you have a source of immense power. The bad news is that you have to really care, it cannot be faked. People somehow know when your passion is forced.

As a leadership tool, passion is commonly misunderstood as meaning a ranting, excessively emotional appeal that sets many people's teeth on edge. In politicians this becomes demagoguery.

The passion that truly works is when you are emotionally connected to what you want to happen. When you make that connection, you sound convincing and others find their emotions become engaged too.

Start by listing your passions. Many of us run away from strong emotions and then wonder why others find us boring or unconvincing. When you use your passion you are also vulnerable, since you are sharing with others what really matters to you. If they reject what you want, in some sense they seem to be rejecting you too.

Passionate leaders are unafraid to let their feelings show. This does not necessarily mean being reduced to a tearful mess, though more than one leader has allowed tears to flow in the passion of the moment.

While passion is now spoken about in businesses more openly, its role can still be misunderstood. Yet its power cannot be denied. US consultant and author Richard Change for example claims these 'tangible, often quantifiable benefits of passion in business

- Provides direction and focus
- Creates energy
- Fosters creativity
- Heightens performance
- Inspires action
- Attracts employees and customers
- Builds loyalty
- Unites the organisation
- Provides a critical edge
- Brings the organisation to a higher plane'

To sum up, passion in leadership is about first becoming absolutely convinced of the importance of what you want to happen and secondly being totally willing to share that strong feeling with others.

TRUST

To inspire people to participate, they need to trust both you and themselves. To engender trust:

- Trust yourself
- Do what you say you will do
- Be reliable
- Trust others

When you trust yourself, you are willing to:

- Listen to that inner voice
- Use your natural instincts
- Allow feelings to play an important, though not necessarily always dominant part in guiding your actions

'The only way to make a man trustworthy is to trust him.'
Henry Stimson, US Secretary of War 1990

The perfect leader builds trust slowly, starting small. For example, you create trust in others when you always do what you say you will do – because effective leaders honour their word. They are consistent in their approach and their policy. Thus leaders partly attract people because they can be relied upon. When you are reliable, people will naturally tend to ask your opinions, seek your help, follow your guidance.

Having developed trust in yourself and shown you trust others, you are ready to move on to helping people learn to trust each other. If you lead a team, for example, this is a crucial part of your job. There may be many creative ways you can discover to engender this trust, some of which may work more quickly than others.

For example, taking your team away for one or two days to focus on how you all work together builds trust. It creates it both between individual team members, and ultimately between the team and the leader. You are unlikely to allow such an investment in team time if you do not first of all trust yourself, and your contribution to the team.

'Trust your hopes, not your fears.'

David Mahoney, chairman, Norton Simon Inc.

Managers who complain that they find it hard to gain people's trust are usually those who have little real faith in themselves and what they want to do. Instead they rely on authority and the power of position to obtain what they want. The trouble is that this way of working is rapidly becoming obsolete.

When you trust other people to perform better than they think they can, you are certainly taking a gamble. It is the kind of gamble, though, that effective leaders take constantly. They rely on others performing beyond their normal limitations, it's how they inspire them, through sharing their expectation that their supporters will do extraordinary things.

Where mutual trust does not exist, people are cautious, less open, less influential, more distant and more inclined to leave at the first opportunity. True leadership is getting ordinary people to do extraordinary things. That's inspirational.

CHAPTER 4

Involvement

Managers devolve, leaders involve. It takes real leadership for people to feel genuinely part of the vision and fully committed to realising it. Too often lip service is paid to the idea of involving people.

James Dyson insists that everyone starting work at his company makes a vacuum cleaner on their first day. This is true from the lowliest member of staff to a non-executive director. 'When you take your self-made vacuum cleaner home' says Dyson you 'get a grasp of the company's *raison d'être*.'

You can rapidly detect a leader who generates a sense of involvement, even when not physically present. In Safeway, for example people confidently talk of 'what Carlos wants' when they have never even met the CEO. Within a year or becoming CEO this inspirational leader had infected the company with his enthusiasm for food retailing, the results of which soon showed up on the bottom line and the company became an attractive target for take over.

In many companies staff seldom contribute to meetings or don't even arrive when invited. Yet companies need people's involvement more than ever, as complexity and specialisation take their toll. High performing leaders generate that sense of involvement, both as a feeling amongst supporters and as a way to make things happen. Like a painter they exploit a colourful palette of leadership actions including:

- Enrolment
- Coaching
- Feedback
- Empowerment
- Personal Investment
- Communication
- Stakeholders

ENROLMENT

In the days of navy press gangs, the trick was to slip a coin into someone's drink. Once the unfortunate person had downed their beer, they had unwittingly 'accepted the King's shilling' and were now legally employed by his majesty's navy. Most press-ganged people though, made poor sailors. At the first chance many deserted so the process had to start all over again.

Trying to force someone's enrolment is like shouting, 'grow' at a plant. While it may sound impressive it is unlikely to achieve much. Effective enrolment occurs when someone 'buys into' what you want to achieve. That is, they take the important step of saying, 'yes, I'd like to be part of that.' In effect they are 'signing on'.

People only 'buy in' or 'sign on' under certain circumstances. To achieve that means discovering how to engage their interest, awaken their curiosity, tap into their ambition, challenge them, arouse enthusiasm, deal with their fears and so on. While leaders often publicly declare the importance of such enrolment employees respond more to actions than words. They want tangible evidence of a real desire for their contribution, rather than token compliance. To deliver this convincingly you need to:

- Communicate your purpose with impact
- Say why you need people's help
- Describe how they can personally affect the outcome
- Invite them to say what they need to feel involved
- Describe how the end result will affect them
- Explain the likely consequences of not enrolling

All these rely on you being a powerful presenter. Most inspirational leaders are outstanding communicators, so if this is your weak area, consider investing in some further training. To assess your readiness to present go to: www.maynardleigh.co.uk/ready.shtml

Apart from putting your message across well, encourage enrolment through directly asking people if they will join with you in the project. You are not asking their permission, just checking that they are with you.

Potential supporters also need to know **why** you require their help. This is not simply about requiring their particular skills. It means wanting them for who they are. Naturally this demands sufficient contact with them to explain just why you believe they are vital to the purpose.

As you enrol people in your projects and they realise the difference their contribution can make, so they can create their own support. Encourage people to do this and you promote a spiral of involvement that will strengthen your effectiveness.

If you are head of a large organisation, making contact with everyone is extremely difficult. You are less convincing at a distance. It always pays to try and do this face-to face with people. Videos, memos, e-mail and other such devices are no substitute for people meeting you personally to hear about the enterprise and learning how much you care about it.

Often though you will have to rely on others to do the communicating for you. This is why your selection of those closest to you is so crucial.

Invite people to say what they require in order to feel enrolled. It might be anything from a hefty salary, to a challenging new role. You can seldom take people's enrolment for granted, even if they have agreed to be employed by you. Try and uncover what they themselves feel would make them committed to the purpose.

Potential supporters want to know ' How will I be affected if I join in?' They may take a great deal on trust. Yet the more you can explain how the end result will affect them, the more you make it easy for them to take that vital first step. Spell out clearly any adverse consequences of not enrolling, such as losing out on important benefits. Avoid making this information into direct threat. Also, if you do paint a thoroughly negative picture of the adverse consequences, be sure it has credibility.

A powerful way leaders obtain enrolment is by enabling people to realise they will be engaged in achieving something extraordinary. How can you expect them to enrol if what is on offer is pedestrian? It must capture their imagination, making them feel that whatever they do they will be traveling towards a worthwhile destination.

Effective leaders develop the knack of explaining how even the simplest tasks link to the grand design.

COACHING

Inspirational leaders coach people at work and sometimes accept coaching for themselves. Being open to coaching is as much a sign of good leadership as being willing to offer it to others. High performing leaders tend to be good coaches. Probably they themselves do not call it that, and there may be no formal coaching sessions. Yet their supporters receive regular guidance that amounts to personal coaching and mentoring. Whether in one-to-one sessions or as part of a group experience, leaders use coaching to involve and steer people in the right direction.

Coaching, therefore, provides an effective way of encouraging performance and demonstrates leadership qualities. Through the resulting relationship, supporters build their confidence to take risks, pursue change and in turn develop their own ability to coach others.

Coaching as a leadership style provides a transition from command and control to a more supportive and facilitative approach. It focuses on developing people, on helping them find their own way to achieve outstanding results. Reasons to start coaching your people include:

- Retention – helps retain talent; increasingly people expect leaders to be willing to coach
- Personal Needs – enables people to find their own way through problem solving and goal setting
- Immediacy – lets you tackle issues as they arise, and manage performance
- Recognition – people want to feel valued and coaching provides personal attention

What is your coaching style and do you feel ready to coach? Check your readiness to coach, at: http://www.maynardleigh.co.uk/inter_coach.shtml

EMPOWERMENT

'When the best leaders' work is done, the people say: "We did it ourselves".'
Lau-Tzu

In simple terms, empowerment means giving people responsibility, the right to make decisions, taking more responsibility for their lives.

Ordering someone to be empowered is a contradiction in terms. Inspirational leadership is about moving from a reliance on control, creating instead an environment that encourages people to take responsibility. When people have the autonomy to take over all aspects of management, including work, holiday scheduling, ordering materials, and hiring new team members, the results are usually spectacular gains in productivity and creativity.

Paradoxically, relinquishing some of your leadership authority may enhance it, because people feel more able to ask for your help, to hear your suggestions and to follow your lead. Some of the results you can expect when your people feel involved are:

- Revitalised employees
- Increased morale
- Increased productivity
- Improved quality
- Lower staff turnover

There are many ways to empower through your leadership. Just be creative in discovering which ones work best for you and your supporters:

- Show people that they are not separate from management and they can help the organisation improve
- Demonstrate convincingly that you implement people's suggestions
- Appreciate and reward suggestions even when they are not implemented
- Trust people with responsibility
- Respect people's ideas and judgment
- Allow people to make decisions

PERSONAL INVESTMENT

Enrolment and empowerment are easier to achieve when people have a personal investment in your vision or purpose. This is not necessarily financial investment. It is a willingness to put more of themselves into the work such as their:

- Time
- Energy
- Creativity
- Ideas
- Know-how
- Personal resources such as information and contacts
- Commitment to personal development and formal training
- Desire to build important work relationships

You don't have to motivate anybody to do something they already want to do. If people are making a personal investment, they become self-motivating, which renders that part of your job redundant. So what is left? Your responsibility to inspire them. For example, in virtual teams – ones that hardly meet and work mainly through electronic means, – leaders rely almost exclusively on tapping into the members' personal investment in the project. They have to somehow create a climate where everyone wants success.

If you want others to make a strong personal investment you must first demonstrate it yourself. It's hard to fake personal investment. People quickly detect when a leader is not wholeheartedly behind something. For example, a chief executive of a London local council habitually made cynical comments about major programmes that he was supposedly pursuing on behalf of his political masters. The results were predictable. Few people believed that he was unreservedly behind the required actions, so they in turn tackled the work by holding back on their best efforts.

- Do a health check on the current personal investment of your supporters

Financially rewarding people for their commitment and involvement also makes good sense. Some companies offer substantial financial incentives for suggestions from individuals. They also offer rewards to teams of employees that have made a collective recommendation. Thus people see tangible evidence that involvement pays.

- Encourage through modeling your own personal investment

FEEDBACK

Actors rehearse and receive continual information about their performance from both their director and ultimately the audience. Musicians look to the conductor both during rehearsals and in the actual performance for guidance on how they are doing.

Leaders are no different. They too need to give and receive continual feedback on how they and others are performing. Inspirational business leaders realise the power of feedback to affect people's performance. They revel in the chance to make these opportunities a creative tour de force in which everyone leaves inspired to perform even better.

Videos of GE's Jack Welch in full flow for instance, show someone using feedback as a strategic weapon in the search for improved performance. Less effective leaders though use such sessions as a form of punishment, hectoring or criticising in the vain hope that it will somehow spur people on. Usually it merely leaves people feeling dispirited.

Some companies make feedback an intrinsic part of their culture, as a sure way to generate higher levels of involvement. For example, as a manager you cannot survive long in FedEx with an adverse six monthly report from colleagues giving feedback on your leadership. A few months later another feedback report had better show an improvement or you may be moved from a leadership role.

Feedback is how people influence your plans and contribute to the vision. Without this essential information you risk being on the receiving end of some possible surprises.

- Ensure that your own performance is continually monitored

Hearing others' opinions is an invaluable resource and the best leaders are hungry to hear what people have to say.

IDENTIFYING STAKEHOLDERS

Inspirational leaders do more than merely inform their stakeholders. They also identify how they need to be involved. Staying closely in touch with stakeholders helps improve the chances of avoiding poor decisions. For example, Shell's leadership fully expected to face the wrath of environmental lobby groups when it tried to dump the Brent Spa oil platform in the North Sea. What it entirely failed to anticipate was that its staff were also stakeholders in the environment. Staff resistance played a major part in reversing the company's unpopular decision.

So leaders who promote involvement tend to ask, 'who are the stake holders, and what do they want?' Mark Feldman and Michael Spratt of PricewaterhouseCoopers, who have studied mergers and acquisitions, found that leaders often resist the idea of getting close to stakeholders and trace this to 'blind arrogance, fear, apathy, ignorance, miserliness, or distrust.'

Start making a list of who benefits, or is involved in some way with what you want to achieve. For instance, if you are the leader of a board of school governors, you have the children, parents, teachers, administrators, unions, governors, council, inspectors and perhaps others who are all part of the well being of the school.

For a leader in a company the list includes staff, customers, directors, shareholders, as well as perhaps local residents, unions, professional associations, and even perhaps charities or community groups who benefit from the company's success. For example, many community groups would be adversely affected if The Body Shop and its leaders began to fail, since the company is deeply involved in supporting local projects.

All such groups may have a part to play in helping to realise your vision. The more you actively involve them, the more energy you have available to get the job done.

It can be both surprising and satisfying to discover that your stakeholders have some strong views on how to help you succeed as a leader. When executives of Asda for example, occasionally stack shelves, they do so alongside people who are low in the pecking order. Yet these people invariably have important insights into how to improve the way the business is run.

'Too bad that all the people who know how to run the country are busy driving taxicabs and cutting hair.'
George Burns, US comedian

Blocks
Naturally there are obstacles to fully involving people. Some of these belong to you, and some to them. Let's start with your own.

A prison governor once declared 'This would be a great place if only we didn't have to fill it with criminals.' For some companies, everything would be fine if only they didn't have to bother with customers. Leaders could say much the same: 'I could be a great leader if only I didn't need supporters.'

It's nearly always a headache dealing with other people and their wants. For leaders and managers it usually feels easier to do many things oneself. That way you don't have to bother allowing for other people's views and their apparent limitations. It nearly always takes more time and energy initially to teach somebody else to do a job, that you know you can do quicker and better yourself.

As a leader you may need to work hard at resisting your natural temptation to keep doing things yourself, and bi-passing your supporters. One of the commonest blocks to being an effective leader is being a control freak – wanting to somehow keep a grip on everything.

The best leaders learn to let go. They continually hand over relevant power and responsibility to others. However they always retain the right to know what is going on.

Another block is your own reaction to hearing what your supporters have to say. Because you know the broader picture, it is all too easy to be resentful or over-confident that you know best.

If you are really going to listen to stakeholders and others, then you may not be able to have everything your own way. That is the price for working collaboratively.

Other people
If you encourage people to be part of your vision, enrol them and obtain their commitment, they may also want some of your power. Otherwise why should they become so involved?

You will almost certainly need to overcome people's natural inertia or apathy, their cynicism, distrust, or resistance. However, this is all part of leading. Your refusal to be dragged down by such negative forces is partly what separates you from supporters.

The difficulties you will face with supporters are part of the job. Leadership is seldom plain sailing and dealing with obstacles, your own and other people's, is what allows you to grow and develop.

IN SUMMARY

Leaders only achieve their dreams through others. When approaching any project, it is worth asking yourself:

- Who else could be involved?
- What specific support can they give me?
- What will they need to be involved (what's in it for them)?
- How can I involve them?

CHAPTER 5

Improvisation

In one of the Indiana Jones films, when the hero is asked about his plan for getting out of trouble, he admits, 'I don't know, I'm just making it up as I go along.' That is why many business leaders are effective too, and why what they do so often differs from more conventional management.

Because something worked last time is no guarantee that it will work again. Like Indiana Jones you need to be willing to invent it as you go along.

Leadership guru, Rosabeth Moss Kanter exploring the notion of strategy as improvisational theatre suggests that it demands a lot of actors. 'The players must be willing to take on unfamiliar roles, think on their feet, pay attention to several things at once, walk into a situation for which they are not prepared and ad lib.' This is how it is for most leaders these days.

Asked for the secrets of improvisation, great stage performers say things like:

- Trust you can do it
- Give yourself permission to experiment and play
- Risk involves failure
- Make failure part of the process – create with it

- Even if what you've just created is good – let go of it, and move on
- Get out of the way – allow your natural talent to perform
- Listen
- Be 'in the moment' – it just went!
- A strong form and structure releases flexibility
- Practice
- Say 'yes' to your colleagues' offerings and work with what they give you
- There are no rules – the above are just guidelines

These are all equally relevant for the inspiratational leader. There are no cast-iron rules of leading. Even if there were, they would certainly alter once you began relying on them. Instead, expand your ability to improvise, to think on your feet, to be creative in any moment, and respond to what is around you. That way you too can do it like it has never been done before. This is how you lead people in a rapidly changing world.

Doing it like it has never been done before is one of the most important aspects of business leadership. When the creator of Federal Express, for example, based the delivery company on a wheel-and-spoke principle, there were many in the industry who had already known and dismissed the concept. Yet none had possessed the courage to put it into effect.

Similarly, the idea of instant and continuous news had been around for years when Ted Turner launched CNN. Many people, in fact, predicted that it would lose a fortune. It took genuine leadership to press ahead regardless, doing what no one else had done so far.

When leaders improvise they use:

- Curiosity
- Creativity
- Flexibility
- Presence

CURIOSITY

Immersed in daily judgments and decisions, leaders can often undervalue the importance of simply being curious. It provides a springboard to leadership creativity.

'It is not easy to be curious,' said Durk Jager when CEO of Procter & Gambol. 'The external environment might favour it, but the culture within most companies does not. Generally, we reward certainty. And we look askance at uncertainty, much less outright confusion. But you have to persevere in the face of such resistance. The pursuit of certainty leads you to a narrow view of the world, and it slows you down in ways no business can afford.'

CREATIVITY

'Resist the usual.'
Raymond Rubicam

We usually think of creativity in simple terms such as being an artist, or perhaps generating lists of new ideas. In fact, leadership creativity is much wider and includes many different aspects of doing things differently. It requires you to:

- Innovate
- Stimulate others

- Create a 'try it' environment
- Problem-solve
- Receive and reward others' ideas

Innovation
'Every act of creation is first of all an act of destruction.'
  Pablo Picasso

Creativity in leadership is not necessarily being innovative yourself, though that certainly helps. It is even more important that you enable others to do it on your behalf. It ought to be in every business leader's job description that they are personally responsible for ensuring the organisation actively encourages innovation, in its many forms.

Innovation often means making something from nothing. Leaders take limited resources and weld them into new combinations, so that something original or different can occur. In business, this mainly happens through identifying key issues and creating powerful teams, project groups, alliances and networks.

The leadership impulse to innovate stems from the drive to initiate – one of the 7 I's of leadership. Doing it successfully depends partly on your own creative process so explore what makes you creative through discovering:

- How do I best tap my natural creativity?
- What triggers my creativity?
- When do I get my ideas?
- How do I usually respond to other people's creativity?
- How often do I take regular time for reflection?

The last of these is much underrated. Standing back and thinking, giving yourself time and space to ruminate and allowing thoughts to wander is not idleness. We need such times. For busy leaders it is particularly hard to obtain them and important that they do.

You can spend weeks or months struggling to force out cost-cutting ideas to save your company money. With time to reflect, you might help produce the answer in ten minutes. By understanding and valuing your own creative process you strengthen your leadership capability.

'A significant number of big money ideas have occurred to me whilst on vacation.'

Nolan Bushnell, entrepreneur/inventor, founder of Atari

Stimulate others

Leadership creativity also stems from enabling others to be inventive and original. Study how to trigger creativity in individuals and teams. Everyone can do it, they may just need a stimulus, and it's your role to provide it.

Discovering what triggers a team's creativity, for example, gives you a powerful tool for making things happen. It is therefore worth learning what works and what does not. Also, people need time to practice being creative, to discover for themselves how best they can do it. Use team meetings to explore creating together. Whether it is brain-storming to tackle a problem, or other creative techniques, every meeting can be a laboratory of invention.

You can set people problems, rotate the chairing role, ask team members to prepare papers and ideas on a subject, suggest they bring in examples of creative work from outside the business – anything to get them buzzing and experimenting.

Your leadership contribution is to provide relevant challenges that stimulate people to find new resources within themselves to create. Even if you genuinely believe they can do this, it is not enough by itself. Communicate it, showing clearly that you have faith in their innate ability to achieve breakthroughs.

A 'try it' environment
At the heart of creativity lies the freedom to experiment and make mistakes. It is a hard freedom for some organisations to tolerate. The drive for fault-free, quality actions may conflict with the right to make mistakes and learn from them.

An important contribution you can make is demonstrating that you want to learn what works through experimentation. By 'modelling' such behaviour you will help others to see the importance of it.

The driving mantra of professional improvisers is 'accept, and build'. It is a guiding principle of improvisation that to be creative with others means accepting their ideas, no matter how crazy, and then building on them. The required response is 'Yes, and . . .' rather than 'Yes, but . . .'

Really effective leaders use every person's contribution as the foundation for possible invention. As a matter of habit they practice accepting ideas and seeing how they can add value to them. They also create an atmosphere where they encourage a 'Yes, and . . .' approach from everyone else.

Practice giving a 'let's try it and see' response, when people produce ideas. This is much preferable to 'Yes but' or 'But' in response to suggestions. People soon learn from your example. When you show that it is all right to experiment, they will tend to convey the same message to others with whom they work.

Underpinning the freedom to experiment are:

- Clarifying the learning
- Not punishing people for mistakes
- Underlining that the only unacceptable mistakes are ones that could 'hole the ship below the waterline'

When you focus on 'what can we learn from this mistake?' rather than 'who's to blame?', you ensure that lessons are not lost for the future. This helps to make your company a 'learning organisation'. Cherish mistakes as invaluable opportunities for learning.

'If I had to live my life again, I'd make the same mistakes, only sooner.'
Tallulah Bankhead

Punishing people for mistakes is a great way to kill off ideas. Once people realise they will suffer retribution when things go awry, they soon learn to play it safe. This is fine if you see an organisation merely as a machine, with the people in it merely cogs. However, this approach is almost certainly bound to fail in our fast-moving world where it is often more important to be flexible than to always get things right.

The freedom to make mistakes is not a licence to be reckless. You do not ignore mistakes by simply shrugging your shoulders and saying 'that's too bad'. Rather, you use them as an opportunity to encourage yet more learning, to get it right next time, to build fail-safe systems.

'An executive who had lost £10 million at IBM was called to meet Thomas Watson Jr, president of the company. "Do you know why you are here?" he asked. "I suppose you're going to fire me?" the anxious executive replied. "Fire you! Are you crazy? I've just spent £10 million on your education."'

Try adopting the principle that people can make mistakes but are not permitted to 'hole the ship below the waterline'. This has stood the test of time. The failure to use it and build sufficient control systems, enabled the maverick dealer Leeson in Singapore to destroy the Barings banking group.

The more you personally commit to the idea of experimentation the better. Involve your team, customers and other stakeholders in your experiments so that they are all sharing the success and any possible failure.

Offer hypotheses for people in the organisation to test. For example, you might suggest that there is a growing market for a new type of service. Presenting this as a hypothesis for testing makes it more likely that you will uncover the truth, rather than having your supporters merely trying to prove you right.

Problem solving

Most work is about solving problems in some form. The more interesting the problem, the more absorbing the work. Most problems are solved easily in the everyday activity of work, using information gained while solving previous problems. Occasionally though, ones arise that are tricky and these tend to get steered towards leaders. Such problems normally have few precedents, requiring a creative response.

We so often spend considerable time worrying about what isn't working rather than putting our attention on what a solution might look like. Imagine how things could be if the problem was overcome. Draw it as a picture or as a symbol. This may help you gain access to the right-hand side of your brain that does not think logically but thinks visually and holistically.

Brain-storming, in which you produce lots of ideas

without initially criticising or rejecting them, can start your natural, subconscious creative powers working. So, involve others and practice 'playing' with the problem. A sense of fun and a lighthearted approach can often release unforeseen solutions for even the most serious difficulties.

Focus on solutions, not obstacles

Receive and reward others' ideas

Companies and teams are full of good ideas, though half of them never get off the ground. As a leader it's your responsibility to find ways of communicating that swiftly move any new idea from source to where it's needed. Suggestion boxes, e-mail systems, open communication – every opportunity can be used to process good ideas so that they can be used quickly.

Many companies have remuneration systems, not just for individuals who have ideas, but for teams throughout the organisation. These can be linked to the profit they create for the organisation. You can create a culture that rewards innovation so that money is used to generate new ideas. However, money is not the only important factor. Equally important is how you and other people receive new ideas. A 'yes' culture responds to new ideas with an open mind: 'yes, we might try that'. Only after this initial response does the more cautious aspect of screening the idea really start.

FLEXIBILITY

'It is an old ironic habit of human beings, to run faster when we have lost our way.'
Rollo May

People have a habit of persistently pursuing actions even when they are patently not getting anywhere. The first rule of holes is: if you're in one, stop digging.

Improvisation is about flexibility. Being able to adjust and adapt to situations is one of our prime abilities as human beings. Flexible thinking lets us resist primitive impulses to carry on regardless of the evidence.

Water is a great symbol of flexible power. If it cannot follow a direct course, it will always find a way through, winding around and adapting to the terrain. Yet its power will always move it onwards.

Clarity

The clearer your vision, purpose or objective, the easier it becomes to be flexible in how you achieve it. Not only may there be many routes to your destination, you may even invent ones that never before existed. By always focusing on the end result, you retain the larger picture. Leaders hold the picture as their guiding star.

'If I don't get there headed straight, maybe I get there by zigzagging, or jumping over the problem.'
Dr. Nathan Kline, psychiatrist and researcher

Openness

Being open to people's ideas can supply you with more choices, some of which may be better than others. Releasing control generates other possibilities. Improvisation creates new solutions. Go with the flow of events, rather than always pushing against them.

When a leader shows flexibility this helps avoid a frenzied reaction to any obstacle, and promotes a creative response. Responding means taking responsibility for using new information and putting it to work.

To respond productively so that you can improvise, you also need to be alert and present.

PRESENCE

Leadership is visibility and Sam Walton's legendary visits to his stores were an inspiration, not just good PR. Leaders who take the trouble to regularly visit different sites, speak to staff and suppliers, offer question and answer sessions, and generally stick around physically, find that it pays huge dividends. Simply 'being there' puts you in a good place to improvise inventive solutions quickly.

For example, John Timpson who ran the national UK chain of shoe repair and service shops often visited his stores and found it had a profound effect on the business. In one case he saw the Cheadle shop displaying a whole line of leather shoes on the rack above the machinery. The manager there repaired more leather-soled shoes than anyone else in the business and his shop was in a small suburb of Manchester. Timpson encouraged every branch to have a similar display of leather shoes and 'in the next eight years, our leather business quadrupled.' No wonder it is called 'walking the talk.'

Leaders who fail to stay present tend to seem on 'auto-pilot'. They appear distracted or aloof, with little interest in what's happening around them. Inevitably this has an impact on others. Gate's notorious videoed court deposition showed him mumbling, evasive and slumped in his chair. He couldn't improvise because, quite simply, he was not 'present'.

So what exactly do leaders do when they demonstrate a presence? First, they are intent on seeing, constantly looking at what's happening now. Secondly, they really listen without apparently planning what to say when their turn comes. They are listening with a clear purpose, in effect mentally checking: 'am I hearing anything that will move us on, how can I contribute to that?'

Thirdly, leaders who are really present stay conscious of their feelings and are willing to use these to guide decisions. Fourthly, they act as if every single moment is different. For example, many talk about 'every minute being an opportunity to move the business on.'

Leaders focus their attention on how they can transform a situation, or create something out of nothing. This implies an intense awareness of moment to moment, a sense of staying conscious to how life changes continuously. It means:

- **Seeing.** Look around at what's happening now; be alert to what's going on; are there opportunities staring you in the face right now?
- **Listening.** We are sometimes so busy planning what we're going to say that we don't listen. True listening is active, not a passive way of waiting for your turn to speak.

  Notice how often you are listening to the voice in your head, rather than fully absorbing what is being said to you. Leaders listen with respect and purpose. They are always asking 'what can I hear that will move us forward and how can I contribute to it?'

  Impressive listening skills have been shown to be one of the common characteristics of credible leaders.
- **Feeling.** Work at becoming more aware of your feelings. These are clues to what excites you and others. Feelings help define: the best decisions, what actions will inspire people, what's going on that others will want to be part of.

SUMMARY

No matter how well we plan, the unforeseen will always threaten our strategy. By actively developing your ability to improvise, you mobilise a whole armoury of new resources to help realise your vision.

CHAPTER 6

Individuality

'Always remember you are absolutely unique.' Commented the renowned researcher and writer Margaret Mead adding the rider, 'just like everyone else.' Being different is a gift we each possess, though not everyone cherishes it like effective leaders do.

Inspirational leaders are unafraid of being different and in most cases revel in it. Paradoxically, they set out to convince people that they are one of them while clearly being personally exceptional. Almost by definition, a leader stands out from others, if only by taking responsibility to lead.

One of the first decisions of a new CEO at EMI who had risen up the ranks was to remove the need to carry internal security passes for moving around the building. This small, apparently insignificant, gesture made a huge impression on people. They saw a human being who understood their needs, an individual stamping his personality on the company and setting the talent free.

Individuals make a difference by being themselves, expressing their own values, beliefs, knowledge and integrity. Although mainly an understated theme, the findings from Jim Collins' seminal study on great companies and their leaders confirm the latter's intense individualism. Because of it they recognise the importance of nurturing individualism amongst all those around them. By contrast the 'genius with a thousand helpers' model, explains Collins, in which the leader sets the vision and then enlists a crew of highly capable 'helpers', tends to fail when the genius departs.

Young, aspiring leaders often try modeling themselves on someone they admire. It is important that you do this in your own way without slavishly imitating whole aspects of a role model's personality. Instead you discover your own uniqueness that will make a difference. Leadership individuality stems from:

- Being Yourself
- Using personal experience
- Style
- Personal values
- Integrity
- Building networks

BEING YOURSELF

Dianne Thompson, a butcher's daughter from Batley became Camelot's Chief Executive and very publicly routed Richard Branson's bid to run the lottery. Michael Grade, a non-executive director of Camelot described her battling away to get the company back in the race for the lottery license: 'She was just herself. There was no PR spin. She believed in the cause, she was a master of the facts and the detail and she spoke intelligently and articulately. She was on top of it. She played a very straight bat and she came over as a real person.'

It is hard to be yourself when all around there are pressures trying to make you into someone else. To fit in, people often sacrifice important distinctive qualities, from frankness to integrity, from sensitivity to humour. To succeed at the top, the pressures to confirm can be even greater.

For example during 2001 the highly successful Operations Director of a well-known UK food company was being groomed to become Managing Director. He was told discreetly that he needed to stop being so ready to say what he thought. To satisfy 'the City' he should start wearing suits. 'I can just see him slowly becoming a grey person. It's like I can see one arm turning grey while the rest of him is still special, soon maybe the rest will follow,' said a close colleague with sadness.

Pressure from the media, the city, your friends, and the organisation, may all conspire to suggest that who you are, is less important than what you do. Yet who you are really matters, it is one of the crucial elements underpinning true leadership. Stelios Haji-Ioannou of Easyjet, Mo Mowlem, James Dyson, Oprah Winfrey, Michael Dell, Lord Brown, Anita Roddick, Ted Turner have all dared to be different and it is their individuality that has helped them triumph.

To be truly yourself is to possess considerable self knowledge, which does not just 'happen'. It occurs because you:

- Are your own best teacher
- Accept responsibilities without blaming others
- Realise that you can learn anything you want to learn
- Reflect on your experiences
- Accept yourself with all your strengths and weaknesses

We can sum these all up as:

- Being true to yourself

'Individuality. . .lies at the heart of all progress'
Gandhi

When you accept who you are, you admire other people without trying to be them. Because Richard Branson for example, walks round in sweaters and casual trousers does not mean everyone who leads a successful business should do the same.

Being distinctive
The more you insist on being yourself, the more distinctive you appear to others. Uniqueness speaks for itself, helping you stand out from the crowd. There is no universal formula for being distinctive. Describing one of Charlemagne's chiefs, someone observed: 'nature made him and then broke the mould.' Each leader does it differently.

The way followers and others talk about a leader usually amount to saying this person is really 'one of a kind'.

Are you prepared to value your distinctiveness? You could be distinctive by how you walk, talk, deal with people, get things done, dress, communicate, define or solve problems, follow your convictions and so on. For example, are you proud of your regional accent or do you try to hide it? Do you love bold colours, yet avoid wearing them because certain people might not approve? If you really believe in something do you say so, or conceal it?

Similarly, when you meet resistance, is your reaction to slow down or back track? Will you risk becoming a target for people jealous of your difference, of your determination to achieve results? Others may not want you stand out, or be antagonised by your refusal to be anonymous. Such is the price of leadership. Are you willing to pay it?

'The thing that makes you exceptional is inevitably that which must also makes you lonely.'
Lorraine Hansberry in, *To be Young, Gifted and Black*

Identity
Effective leaders possess a clear sense of their personal identity, linked to what they want – their destiny. Who they are defines what they want to achieve.

A clear sense of who you are lets you take risks, and step out. Believing that whatever you do never fundamentally alters your essential self means you are secure in your personal identity. You carve your own route and avoid over compliance.

'To be authentic is literally to be your own author, to discover your own native energies and desires and then to find your own way of acting on them.'
Warren Bennis, leadership expert

There is no short cut to achieving a strong personal identity. It's a journey of many years and you are already on it. However, you can choose to:

* Stay aware of your journey
* Seek experiences that test and strengthen your identity

PERSONAL EXPERIENCE

You are responsible for your own development and personal growth. No organisation can commit enough time or resources to you. The Human Resources department will only go so far in providing you with opportunities and training situations. It will never be quite enough.

Do you have some kind of a personal plan to develop yourself and provide yourself with the kind of personal experience that will increase your effectiveness as a leader? If you do not make one, probably no one else will. Even if they do, you are the only one really committed to making it work.

You already bring a wealth of personal history to the job of leading. Often this experience may have had little directly to do with actually leading. For example, your ability to understand and empathise with other comes from having shared similar experiences.

If people around you are facing chaos, success, loss, uncertainty, triumph, despair – you are more able to lead them through these periods if you have encountered similar experiences. Our personal history provides us with rich resources to deal with current problems.

We are also much more than just our history. While past experience has value, in our fast changing world, it may prevent us taking a fresh look at what is happening around us. Leaders approach each new situation with an enquiring mind, a readiness to do things differently.

The best leaders abandon old ideas and provide first a shock and then an inspiration for their followers. When Alexander cut the Gordian knot, rather than trying to unravel it, he was refusing to let past experience dictate how he solved the problem. His solution has inspired people ever since. Despite years of imprisonment, Nelson Mandela refused to allow bitterness to colour his approach to dealing with those who had imprisoned him. This transformed the negotiations that eventually led to him becoming president of South Africa. It inspired some of his strongest enemies who came to see him as an acceptable leader.

How can you capitalise on your personal experience? One simple way is to always conduct a debriefing of every project, big or small. Dissect every failure, not to apportion blame, but to answer a simple question:

- 'What can I learn from this?'

Study individuals like you who have already mastered the skills you need. It could be running a meeting, giving inspiring presentations, making a sale, conducting an interview. How could you acquire such mastery? What personal experiences will you need so as to became a master at it too?

PERSONAL STYLE

'To live is not just to survive, but to thrive with passion, compassion, some humour and style.'
Maya Angelou

Inspirational leaders generally have a distinctive style that other people immediately recognise. In marketing terms they are a 'brand'. This might ultimately reduce to a pattern of consistent and recognisable behaviour. It might be appearance, as with Branson and his no-tie policy or John Harvey Jones with his flowery ties. It might be Bill Gates with his refusal to engage in any kind of small talk. Yet the outward appearance merely reflects who they are as people. These individuals do not wear 'costumes' solely for effect, though they clearly have an impact. They do it because this is partly how they express themselves and assert the ways in which they are special.

'How do you see my particular style?' can be a sobering question for any leader to pursue. The words people use, and the images they evoke, all convey your leadership style and whether it is a source of inspiration.

Understanding how you come across to other people, means exploring both the good and the bad elements of your style. There is your ability to listen, communicate clearly, get things done. Other aspects of your style may be less inspiring, such as your impatience, your lateness for meetings, your loss of the big picture when under pressure and so on.

The strongest part of your style may be something that you least recognise or even value. Perhaps it is your humour or your caring that people find appealing about you as a potential leader. Only if you know and acknowledge these assets can you capitalise on them.

It can be confusing to try and separate your essential style from how people view you in your formal role. So, truly effective leaders want feedback from outside sources that see reality. Enlightened Kings for instance hired advisers and traveling philosophers from foreign lands, or visited them in their own territory.

Today's forward-thinking business leaders visit colleagues in different organisations, use outside consultants and adopt personal effectiveness coaches to offer them a different truth from the one readily on the lips of subordinates.

Your personal style provides freedom for you to be the opposite of how you are normally seen, without losing yourself. For example, if you are generally pleasant and smiley you have plenty of room to be occasionally tough and uncompromising. Similarly, if you tend to be a rather serious, thoughtful person, you have scope to be exactly the opposite, without being immediately dismissed as frivolous.

Although we recognise people for their achievements we also recall *how* they did it. A leader's style says a lot about who they are and what they stand for. As author Martin Amis puts it: 'Style is not neutral; it gives moral directions.'

PERSONAL VALUES

Values, both those that we approve and those that we don't, have roots as dep as creosote rings, and live as long and grow as slowly.'
Wallace Stegner, Writer

Unlike Groucho Marx who joked: 'I have principles and if you don't like them, I have others', inspirational leaders express their individuality through strong personal values and manifest integrity. Who you are and what you stand for governs the way you lead and what you can hope to achieve.

Inspirational leaders are willing to take a stand. They have a point of view and bring their personal experience to bear on issues. People turn to them for advice because they recognise a broad, sometimes world perspective and someone drawing on a distinctive set of personal values. They also share their views.

There is nothing esoteric about values. They are simply what you care about, what you value most. In a people-centered organisation, for instance, showing your humanity directly connects to being an effective leader.

Leaders who suffer the most stress seem to be those who consign their compassion to their social life, whilst maintaining a hard-nosed ruthlessness in the workplace. Inspirational leaders seldom compartmentalise in this way. Instead they bring the whole of themselves to the organisation. This willingness to be a complete person, to take a stand actually builds leadership integrity. When you remain consistent in your commitment to certain basic principles, people come to rely on and trust them.

What most matters to you? You will find the answers in your work, your possessions and your relationships. Try reviewing all three. Can you identify the values that matter? Are these of use to other people? Are your values mainly positive or negative in their outlook. Destructive values for example, will be unlikely to gain widespread support.

'The trouble with the rat race is that even if you win, you're still a rat.'
Lily Tomlin

Could you explain your personal values to other people? Everyone knew what Ghandi stood for, while one of the complaints about President Bush Snr was that he apparently had no strongly held beliefs. Business leaders become well known, not merely through their commercial successes, but also because they constantly clarify what they stand for, what matters to them.

- Write out your personal credo or what matters to you
- Spend time clarifying your values
- Make your values visible by behaving consistently with them

Being consistent with your values is where the phrase 'walk the talk' comes from. It means if you value quality, for instance, then it appears in everything you do; if you value people, you are seen as caring, someone who spends time with them. If you value efficiency, lead the way by being highly efficient yourself.

Having clear and powerful values allows you to bounce back after setbacks. Because you know what you stand for, you are not deterred or undermined by failure. Instead you merely use it to learn from and press onwards towards realising your vision.

The process of getting clear about your values is time-consuming, hard and never really stops. Invent your own ways of focusing on values, making them explicit, sharing them and keeping them high profile.

By constantly talking about your personal values you show you know your own mind. When you are faced with uncertainty or risk, your values enable you to proceed without direction or even approval from someone in authority. When as a leader you successfully share these values with others you begin to help them make decisions and act independently.

Although values may sound a vague concept, people soon understand what you mean and will usually welcome your attempts to clarify them. When you engage in a dialogue about values, people develop a sense of their own and others' position. The discussions could be about how you value customers, what is the most appropriate return to shareholders, how best to satisfy certain stakeholders and so on.

Talking about values brings them alive. Your supporters will be filled with energy and enthusiasm if you speak with passion about those values you both share.

INTEGRITY

'It takes 20 years to build a reputation and five minutes to ruin it. If you think about that, you'll do things differently.'
Warren Buffet

This is the single characteristic most often mentioned as essential for leadership in studies of managers. That is, being someone who is truthful, trustworthy, with character and convictions.

Integrity is normally defined as meaning moral soundness and probity, yet the word comes from wholeness and completeness – a person who has integrated their values and their actions. Leaders without it are usually destructive, and untrustworthy. They seldom achieve credible long-term high performance, because they lack a mature wholeness and consistency.

Leaders with integrity have personal values running through their whole being like a gold seam. It's possible to survive a long time without showing much integrity – the notorious Robert Maxwell for example managed to avoid it for years, but his deceit and duplicity eventually caught up with him.

'Integrity is the essence of everything successful.'
R. Buckminster Fuller

Company scandals such as Enron, Anderson, and the like have merely highlighted the importance of having leaders with a personal commitment to integrity. In the case of Enron it had clear company values, including integrity and these were were strung up in banners at the company headquarters. Yet its leaders acted entirely at odds with them.

As a leader, personal integrity means you:

- Uphold agreements
- Honour contracts
- Keep your word

Leaders who constantly break their word, seldom last or are remembered mainly with distaste. Gone are the days when leaders were meant to be superior beings, high-flown and haughty. These days, leaders need to be seen as real, down to earth and fully rounded human beings.

By knowing yourself sufficiently well, you become able to accept who you are. It is this honesty integrated into all aspects of yourself that produces integrity. It is why you will appear consistent to others.

'The secret of success is consistency of purpose.'
Benjamin Disraeli

NETWORKS

You will notice that one 'I' missing from our 7 I's of leadership is *isolation*. So many leaders succeed because of their wide personal contacts. They have a huge network of people from whom they draw information, advice, and challenge. It is a vital factor in helping them pursue their goals efficiently.

Often leaders are invited to join an organisation mainly because they bring with them a whole list of personal contacts. If you are an organisational leader in a major company try asking yourself:

- Do I know a hundred people who I can personally trust to gain honest help and advice?

Or if you're someone just starting a business try asking yourself.

- Do I personally know a hundred people who would be interested in my product or service?

The chapter on Involvement highlights how productive it is to gain as many participants as possible in your schemes and project. They lend you a mass of energetic support. The same goes for your personal network of friends, colleagues and acquaintances.

Building networks does not mean developing relationships simply to extract business from them. Nor does it mean manipulating people to advance your career. Respected leaders usually develop these contacts from a genuine desire to make friends with people. Their natural gregariousness and wish to participate, help generate networking.

Like any relationship you need to work at networking. You cannot ignore someone for years and then expect them to perform favours when you contact them out of the blue. Nurture your contacts, spend time looking after them. Seek opportunities to help them out when you can. Pass on ideas or information if you feel it will support them. The more you put out, the more you will get back.

CHAPTER 7

Implementation

As an inspirational leader you need to become an implementation expert. There can be no hiding behind the idea that 'I'm great on strategy but others need to handle the details.' Ultimately you succeed in your role when you deliver results which means you need to be involved in follow through.

As a leader you are there mainly to make something happen. It is not enough to be a wonderful human being, with terrific style and integrity, who treats people well. People will support you because they want to contribute to what you want to achieve.

'Well done, is better than, well said.'
Benjamin Franklin

Successful leaders are therefore experts in delivery. While it is important to have a mastery of rhetoric and a powerful communication style this is merely the starting point. To be a leader who is strong on implementation people need to see you:

- Be action-minded
- Model behaviour

- Demand feedback
- Persevere
- Celebrate success

ACTION MINDED

'Whatever you can do or dream you can, begin it. For boldness has genius, power and magic in it. Begin it now!'
Goethe

What makes inspirational leaders so unstoppable? Typically they share an obsession for making things happen, sometimes at almost any price. They are only too aware that ideas, vision and plans become meaningless when people do not see the leader pushing hard for action.

The push begins when you constantly talk about the priorities, what has to be done and by when. For example, a new chief executive in one company took the decision to sell off its restaurants chain. He announced to the top team they had just one year to make it happen. Two months later in a meeting with him, one of the team pointed out there was only a year left to complete the sale. The CEO replied that in fact there was now only 10 months left. The next day for the first time there was real energy around the task in hand.

'Just do it.'
Nike Corporation

- Talk about what you want to achieve – endlessly.

Be willing also to devote apparently limitless energy to ensuring your words are turned into deeds. Leaders seldom initiate witch hunts or waste time justifying why things have not happened. They are far more concerned with the future, on making it happen.

'Someone's sitting in the shade today because someone planted a tree a long time ago.'
Warren Buffet

Deeds
Focus on deeds, rather than rhetoric. While it is certainly important that you are persuasive verbally, ultimately people want to know: 'Yes, but what do you want us to do?'

Without a strong focus on deeds you risk being seen only as a prophet or visionary, rather than a leader. Inspirational leaders have a preference for action, usually at the expense of discussion or prolonged debate.

'The activist is not the man who says the river is dirty. The activist is the man who cleans up the river.'
H. Ross Perot, founder of EDS and Perot Systems.

Make Decisions
Lack of decision taking often explains why some leaders never make a real difference. However, inspirational leaders usually prefer them to be made by those responsible for implementing them. They encourage people to have:

- The necessary information on which to base decisions
- Adequate training to recognise when a decision is needed
- The ability to distinguish a good decision from a bad one
- A desire to learn from past decisions

Inexperienced leaders wonder what people will think of them and their performance if they do not personally keep making decisions and delivering answers. Typically the fear is that 'I'll lose their respect' or 'I won't be seen as earning my salary.' Yet if people are busy enjoying their jobs they seldom think such things and realise that an effective leader is there to serve them, to help them do their own work better.

'Most of our executives make very sound decisions. The trouble is many have then not turned out to be right.'
Donald Bullock training director of C&P Telephone Company

When it's your call on a decision, take time to reflect and avoid being pressured into the wrong choice. Set a definite limit for when you must decide. While it is important to weigh up alternatives and see all sides of an issue, this is no substitute for actually choosing.

Think and communicate with purpose
As we saw earlier, creative thinking is an important stimulus and source of leadership action. Such thinking deals with newness, the future, and with challenging the way things are always done. To monitor your own creative thinking start noticing:

* Are my thoughts mainly focused on action?
* Do I prefer rehearsing history, rather than focusing on the future?
* Am I willing to question the 'rules' or rock the boat?

'Few people think more than two or three times a year. I have made an international reputation for myself by thinking once or twice a week.'
George Bernard Shaw

How much of your daily communications contain a purpose that demands action, rather than just discussion? Try keeping a check for a week to discover how much you moan about what's wrong or attempt to justify mistakes. Inspirational leaders avoid such unproductive behaviour.

Follow through

Golfers and tennis players put full power into a shot by allowing the swing to follow-through, *after* hitting the ball. This seems odd. How on earth can hitting it well be affected by what you do afterwards? The explanation is that contact with the ball is only part of an effective shot.

All actions have a wider context. In your case they are part of your broader vision. The golfer uses a mental picture of hitting the ball to a certain place and physical follow-through of the swing helps get it there. Likewise, your own vision for your team or organisation requires certain actions or follow-through en route.

Follow-through by an action-minded leader means asking questions like:

- How are things going?
- What is happening?
- What's the news?
- Tell me the latest?
- Give me an update?

The more intense the follow-through, the more powerful the associated actions become. For example, keep asking people 'what happened after we talked, or made a decision, or started that project, or hired that new person?' Do this in an interested way, rather than pestering them, or making them feel you are checking up on them.

Often leaders invent opportunities where others have only seen information or facts. The difference is their determination to stay action-minded, rather than becoming immersed in data.

Completion

The world is full of people with half-finished projects and ideas that never quite happened. Inspirational leaders are sound implementers who either:

- Follow through to completion, or;
- Formally abandon a possible course of action

Get clear on which of these you are pursuing at any particular moment. This helps other people clarify in their own minds what they should do. By following through to completion you create space for something else to happen. Uncompleted projects, tasks and paper work sap energy simply by hanging around, seemingly demanding your attention. To deal with these:

- Set definite deadlines for finishing
- Identify areas of your work filled with irrelevancies
- Check your physical work space and remove unnecessary clutter

The more you can clear space in your environment and your life, the more you enable new opportunities to arise.

Smart goals

A particularly useful way of identifying practical actions is the SMART goal system. There are various versions of this acronym but the version we prefer is:

- Stretching – a person's reach should exceed their grasp; unchallenging goals seldom work
- Measurable – make goals specific, so you know whether or not they are achieved and at what rate
- Agreed – ensure goals are realistic and accepted by people rather than just imposing them
- Recorded – keep track of events so that you know what is supposed to be achieved and by whom
- Time limited – put a time boundary around the aim so that people are working to understandable deadlines

Asking for help

Inspirational leaders don't do it alone. They are intensely aware of needing supporters. Observe a talented leader and you might wonder why they are so successful since they seem to need so much help! They keep asking everyone around them for it.

For some people asking for help is difficult. At the risk of generalising, why is it that so many men drivers who are lost hate asking for directions, while women seem more happy to do so? Admitting that you are lost or confused can be also be a cultural issue, with an unwillingness to show weakness. Many traditional managers for example, baulk at the idea of revealing they don't have the answers. Successful leaders though are less precious about showing they need help to implement their dreams.

Balance
While it is essential to focus on action, be wary of:

- A manic dash for constant activity
- Losing the big picture

There is a difference between leadership energy and frenetic activity where you never seem to sit still. This is a sign of someone trying to do it all themselves. Leaders who do too much, lead for only a short time before they burn out.

MODEL BEHAVIOUR

'Example is leadership'
Albert Schweitzer

A group of senior managers at Barclays Bank on a development workshop set a goal for the future quality of their presentations. They agreed that they wanted to be 'as good at presenting as our CEO, Matt Barrett.' Talented people want to be around leaders they can emulate as well as admire.

Modelling speaks louder than words. You gain leadership credibility through practicing what you preach. When you set an example, people believe what you say, and start trying to emulate your example.

You are coaching when you show through your own actions what you expect from someone else. It is far more convincing than exhortations and is an enormously powerful tool. You cannot lead from behind and expect people to be other than cynical about your leadership.

- Nothing undermines a leader, more than suggesting 'do as I say, not as I do.'

When you lead by example, you become highly visible. Outstanding leaders do not need to be show-offs, but they are willing to be seen, and held accountable. There is no hiding as a leader, particularly in an age of rapid change and almost instant communications.

Do you hate public attention and news about how you come across? If so, you will automatically reduce your impact. Successful leaders do not allow their frail egos to prevent them from putting themselves and their ideas into the world. You don't have to do it in a brash way, but being a leader is being upfront.

When you lead by example you:

- Share your vision
- Promote your values
- Show commitment to achieving results

It is easy to underestimate the power of modelling. Yet it achieves far more than exhortation. Mere words about what you want to achieve, soon bores potential supporters into looking elsewhere for inspiration. They want help converting the rhetoric into practical tasks. They need to understand how to play a real part in achieving the vision.

'Leaders must be seen to be upfront, up to date, up to their job and up early in the morning.'
Lord Seiff of Marks and Spencer

An absence of modelling invariably separate managers from true leaders. It is far easier to issue tablets from the mountain than show the way yourself. Not believing in something makes modelling it yourself into a terrific strain. How can you convincingly show what is required if you are not emotionally, as opposed to just intellectually, committed to it?

Meetings are an important place in which to demonstrate modelling. This is where leaders spend much of their time and how you behave during them sends important messages throughout the entire organisation. People expect you to:

- Communicate clearly and succinctly
- Be open to suggestions
- Listen attentively
- Make sure everyone is involved
- Keep a tight hold on time

This kind of behaviour sets the standards for others to follow.

FEEDBACK

Inspiration leaders are experts at both giving and receiving feedback. They refuse to do without it and are tenacious at maintaining it both ways. You can only know how you are performing as a leader through frank and perhaps challenging feedback. Perhaps one of the toughest demands on a leader is to stay open to being judged by others.

The faster a car goes, the greater the wind resistance. Similarly, the more action you take, the more 'flak' you are likely to attract. You are bound to meet some objections to your plans, hit natural resistance, face disbelief or incomprehension. Feedback tells you about these reactions so that you respond appropriately. You need negative and positive kinds for implementing your vision.

But feedback only makes real sense in relation to some goal. 'How am I doing' for example makes little sense without knowing in relation to what? You can give and receive regular feedback in many ways:

- Informal conversations
- Formal sessions such as performance reviews
- Coaching
- Mentoring

Informal conversations

Successful leaders build personal networks to ensure their information stems from a diversity of sources. Informal feedback opportunities are everywhere, you just have to take advantage of them. Even a chat in a lift may yield precious data about how you are performing or the progress of your plans.

Formal Sessions

Within most organisations there are usually several types of formal mechanisms for obtaining feedback. Ensure there are formal feedback mechanisms available to serve both you and your supporters. These might include appraisals, briefings, team meetings, consultation sessions and so on.

Coaching

Who do you turn to for support? While you can expect some help from those you lead, it is important as a leader to avoid 'dumping' on people, forcing them to hear your personal troubles, fears and worries about what you are trying to achieve. This does not mean you over-protect them from the truth or issues that might affect them. It does mean being thoughtful in how you share what you are up against as an inspirational leader.

Consider finding a coach who offers a fresh perspective to your work, someone who understands that what matters to you is achieving your vision. Your coach can be someone outside the organisation, or even someone who does not know much about your business or job. Whoever you choose it should be someone you can respect, who can bring different ideas to the conversation and offer new information and perspectives.

Mentoring

Occasionally it is useful to work with someone who is not merely a coach but someone you admire for how they get results. A mentor might be someone senior in your organisation, or your industry, or they could be in an entirely different industry, or even part of the world. You may only see the mentor occasionally, but he or she is available to you for advice and help.

It is a sign of strength, not weakness, to adopt a mentor. It means that you are open to new ideas, to developing yourself, and learning from somebody who perhaps has more experience than you.

Contacting the right mentor is seldom easy. You are looking for someone unusual, who you can admire and respect. A good mentors will avoid giving you direction, or solve your problems with a simple answer, acting instead more as a sounding board.

PERSEVERANCE

'Press on. Nothing in the world can take the place of persistence.'
Ray Croc, founder of McDonald's

'They struggle very hard and keep on persisting. They enjoy their work. They excel at concentrating and persevering.' Professor Michael Howe of Exeter University speaking at the annual conference of the British Psychological Society in April 2000 was referring to geniuses. Yet he might equally have been describing inspirational leaders, rather than the likes of Isaac Newton, Darwin and Einstein.

Explaining the genius phenomenon, Howe found that 'what makes them special is their long-term commitment. Their efforts are focused and all geniuses have a firm sense of direction.' The inspirational leader too believes in what he or she wants and persists at it, seldom giving up.

While persistence and even obstinacy can make perfect sense for a leader wanting to implement change and make things happen, it can also spiral into unreasoning pig- headedness. Lord Simpson's determination to push ahead and get rid of Marconi's defence capabilities, despite warnings that it was selling the family silver, led to corporate disaster. Marks and Spencer's commercial ventures in America and France persisted unprofitably until an entirely new leadership grasped the nettle and brought them to an abrupt end.

Sheer persistence though can eventually becomes a source of inspiration. In the popular film *Forest Gump*, the hero's endless running across America eventually attracts a dedicated band of followers attracted by his perseverance. They don't even know exactly why he's running, only that he never seems to stop. Sheer persistence often sets leaders apart from other people. They continue long after others have given up, abandoned hope or lost enthusiasm.

It is hard to keep going as a leader sometimes. That is why it can be so important to have support, involve others and create networks. While the more passionate you are about your vision the more likely you are of achieving it, there will always be moments of self doubt, or concern about the obstacles. During such times you dig deep inside yourself to find that extra bit of commitment to persist.

Dogged determination is not something you can learn – but you can practice it. This is when you need to tap those personal sources of inspiration mentioned earlier in Chapter Three.

'I had to pick myself up and get on with it, do it all over again, only even better this time.'
Sam Walton, founder of Wal-mart.

CELEBRATION

'If you want something to grow, pour champagne on it,' says Carol Lavin Bernick president of Alberto Culver in North America. 'We've made a huge effort – maybe even an over the top effort – to celebrate our successes, and indeed just about everything we'd like to see happen again.'

Inspirational leaders realise the importance of celebration. They search for excuses to party, to remind people that things are going well, or to publicly recognise individual achievements. Leaders often know full well how celebrations inspire people.

Yet emotionally many leaders seem inhibited from promoting celebration or even participating in it wholeheartedly. If you find it hard to promote celebration, consider having someone close to you who loves to party and keep asking them about the opportunities. You can't exactly out-source celebration but you can make sure it constantly happens under your leadership.

Sometimes simply turning up and showing that you care about what people have achieved will be more than enough to make a real impact. Make sure you stay informed about when your people have triumphed and celebrate their success.

Don't wait for some formal opportunity to celebrate, grab the opportunities when you can. For example, if you think people have done something exceptional, rather than waiting for a grand occasion to say so, consider giving everyone some time off, there and then so you can all go somewhere exciting to celebrate.

By breaking goals into manageable steps, you provide milestones when people can, in effect pause and admire the view. Ask them to help identify these and how they would like to celebrate reaching each one.

Find ways of identifying corporate achievement – end of year figures, new contracts, faultless administration, quality production, exceptional customer feedback – and celebrate these. When you start taking these kinds of achievements for granted you will be starting to diminish your leadership impact.

Uncover your own appropriate style of encouraging celebrations. While it may not be razzmatazz, people do need to know what success feels like. It gives them a taste and hopefully makes them want more.

AND FINALLY

The seven I's of leadership: Insight, Initiative, Inspiration, Involvement, Improvisation, Individuality, and Implementation can help you achieve your vision.

Leadership is not an easy burden, although it is a vital one. The world needs leaders. Our planet and the people who live here are in dire need of people with the imagination and inspiration to help create a better world. You personally can make a difference. There are a lot of people out there waiting for you.

'Our deepest fear is not that we are inadequate. Our deepest fear is that we are powerful beyond measure. It is our light, not our darkness that most frightens us. As we let our own light shine, we unconsciously give other people permission to do the same. As we are liberated from our own fear, our presence automatically liberates others.'

Quoted by Nelson Mandela 1994 in his Inaugural Speech.

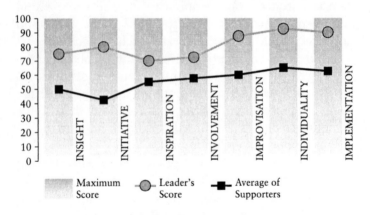

THE 7 I'S LEADERSHIP PROFILE

Many leaders have enjoyed exploring their leadership impact using the 7 I's leadership profile. You select up to five Supporters who experience your leadership and who you trust to provide frank and fair comment on your impact. Supporteres can be anywhere inside or beyond your organisation.

Sample Leadership Profile summary report

		Leader's Score	Supporters' Average	Variations
INSIGHT				
Self awareness	Q1 Seems constantly aware of how he/she is feeling and the impact it has on others	86%	86%	0
Understanding others	Q2 Has a good understanding of what others are thinking and feeling	72%	86%	+14
Seeing the situation	Q3 Is alert to external factors and their possible impact on our organisation	72%	77%	+5
INITIATIVE				
Taking responsibility	Q4 Readily offers to be accountable for achieving something	86%	77%	-9
Risk	Q5 Looks for opportunities to do new things, even when unsure of the final outcome	58%	77%	+19
Adding value	Q6 Promotes changes that add value to our business	72%	81%	+9
Vitality	Q7 You really sense this person's energy and aliveness	86%	91%	+5
INSPIRATION				
Vision	Q8 Has a clear picture of what should happen in the future	86%	72%	-14
Communication	Q9 Talks openly and clearly about what he/or she thinks	86%	72%	-14
Passion	Q10 Is highly committed and cares strongly about his/her beliefs	72%	86%	+14
Excitement	Q11 Excites people to go in the right direction	58%	91%	+33

A detailed numerical report analysing each aspect of the elements making up the 7 I's compares your view of your leadership impact with those of your chosen supporters. The results also come in chart form.

More details are shown at:
www.maynardleigh.co.uk/7i_profile_services.shtml
This is a paid for service.

For more tips and to complete a 7 I's Leadership Profile visit: www.maynardleigh.co.uk

The 7 I's of Leadership

 INSIGHT
- Self-awareness
- Understanding others
- Seeing the situation

 INITIATIVE
- Taking responsibility
- Risk
- Direct action
- Vitality

 INSPIRATION
- Vision
- Communication
- Passion
- Trust

 INVOLVEMENT
- Enrolment
- Empowerment
- Personal investment
- Feedback

 IMPROVISATION
- Creativity
- Flexibility
- Presence

 INDIVIDUALITY
- Being yourself
- Personal experience
- Style
- Values
- Integrity
- Networking

 IMPLEMENTATION
- Action-minded
- Modeling
- Feedback
- Perseverance

Read on for details of new editions of the bestselling *Perfect* series now available from Random House Business Books

PERFECT PRESENTATION

Andrew Leigh and Michael Maynard

Many people are terrified of making a presentation in public, while others are just unsure of how to go about it effectively. But the ability to do it successfully can make all the difference to your personal career, and to the business prospects of your firm. This book provides a sure-fire method based on the 5 P's of Perfect Presentation: Preparation, Purpose, Presence, Passion and Personality. It is an excellent, hands-on-guide which takes the reader step by step to success in one of the most important business skills.

£6.99   1 844 13020 7

PERFECT CAREER

Max Eggert

In a world where job opportunities are continually shrinking it is more important than ever before to actively manage your career. More time is spent at work than in any other activity, so it is vital to make sure that you are following the correct path.

Perfect Career adjusts the balance in your favour, first by helping you to make a thorough analysis of your skills, experiences and values, and then providing practical strategies to enable you to achieve your career ambitions.

£6.99   1 8441 3145 9

PERFECT CV

Max Eggert

Whether you're applying for your first job or planning an all-important career move, your CV is the most potent strike weapon in your armoury. This classic, bestselling book is a concise and invaluable guide that gives you the blueprint for the perfect CV. It shows you clearly and quickly how to present you and your skills and experience in the best possible way – and how to avoid the many easily-made mistakes which swiftly antagonize potential employers.

£6.99   1 8441 3144 0

PERFECT INTERVIEW

Max Eggert

Perfect Interview is comprehensive, but concise and to-the-point. It shows you quickly and clearly how to present yourself and your skills in the best possible way at an interview. Packed with success, tips and checklists, it will enable you to make sure the interview goes the way *you* want it to – and that the result is a job offer that's satisfactory to both you and your new employer.

£6.99   1 8441 3143 2